WILLIAM
HORDERN

CHRISTIANITY
COMMUNISM
and HISTORY

ABINGDON PRESS
New York • *Nashville*

CHRISTIANITY, COMMUNISM, AND HISTORY

Library of Congress Catalog Card Number: 54-7029

SET UP, PRINTED, AND BOUND BY THE
PARTHENON PRESS, AT NASHVILLE,
TENNESSEE, UNITED STATES OF AMERICA

To

My MOTHER
and FATHER

ACKNOWLEDGMENTS

I WISH to express my deepest gratitude to many persons whose contributions made this book possible.

In the first place, there are my former teachers at Union Theological Seminary—Reinhold Niebuhr, John C. Bennett, Frederick C. Grant, and Robert Handy—who helped me in the first research that was ultimately to lead to this work. None of them can be held responsible for the form or opinions of the present work, but without their early help it would not have been written.

Mrs. S. M. Foster and Mr. Robert Schroeder worked patiently to make available to me the riches of the McAlpin Collection of sixteenth-century books at Union Theological Seminary Library. The librarians of the Friends Library at Swarthmore College performed a similar service.

My former professor D. S. Dix, of St. Andrew's College, Saskatoon, Canada, gave me the inspiration and vision that motivated me to the further study that made it possible to write this book. Like all his students, I owe more to his inspiration and leadership than can be expressed.

A special word of gratitude must go to my wife, who helped to prepare the manuscript and bore with me during the writing of it.

CONTENTS

INTRODUCTION

MANY men have helped to change the course of history, but no two have more completely disrupted the ways of man than Jesus Christ and Karl Marx. Jesus Christ, a carpenter, lived two thousand years ago and was crucified while still young. Karl Marx, an intellectual bourgeois, was born in 1818 and died in 1883 as he sat quietly in a chair, long years after he had been hounded out of his native land by governmental oppression. Both men were attacked for destroying religion, and yet both founded new religions, Christianity and Communism. Jesus built his religion upon peace, love, and brotherhood; Marx built his upon revolution, class war, and the fraternity of the proletariat. Today these two religious systems face each other in the world. No other force can rival them. The problem of comparing is difficult because each is today a perversion of the ideals of its founder. Yet the comparison must be made.

KARL MARX, THE ENIGMA

Marx is an enigma, a man of paradox. He was a striking figure at whom one would look twice in passing. His large forehead, ferocious beard, unkempt clothes, and flashing eyes drew attention. For years he sat, a recluse, buried in research as he filled the room with a haze of cheap-cigar smoke. He passed almost unknown in the world of his day, and yet *Time* magazine (by no stretch of the imagination a supporter of

11

Marx's views) calls him the man of the twentieth century.[1] He preached a philosophy of materialism, claiming that the struggle for the material things of life was the basic force in history. But he lived a life that would do credit to the most idealistic ascetic. He turned his back upon the position and wealth that his genius might have won for him and lived on the border line of poverty for the sake of his faith. He struggled to make socialism scientific by fighting all utopianism and stripping the social struggle of its moral elements. Yet today his science is discredited and obsolete, but his picture of a classless society is a utopian heaven that calls millions to action and hope.

Marx attacked the capitalistic economic system, but he kept from starvation by living on the income of Engels' capitalist father. Thus Arthur Koestler says, "Marx [was] a pathologically quarrelsome old sponger," [2] and there is an element of truth in the statement.

Marx was a fighter against all orthodoxies, and yet there has been formed in his name the most orthodox-conscious of all modern societies. The Communist Party of Russia "physically liquidates" any who are guilty of even the slightest heresy if they are politically dangerous and sharply reprimands all scientists, musicians, and writers whose works deviate the smallest fraction from the Party line. The Communist Party throughout the world has again and again been split into factions, each declaring that it alone is orthodox. It has been claimed that if Christ had returned in later centuries, he would have been crucified anew by those who called themselves Christian. There can be little doubt that if the free-thinking,

[1] Feb. 23, 1948.
[2] The Yogi and the Commissar, and Other Essays (New York: The Macmillan Co., 1945), p. 68.

authority-criticizing Marx should appear in modern Russia, the best he could hope for would be a Siberian labor camp.

Nonetheless, Marx is the man of the century, as *Time* magazine suggests. No nation can ignore the results of his thinking. In his name whole societies have been built, and other societies are in debt to him to a greater degree than they might like to admit at this stage of world affairs. Yet Marx would, on the basis of his own theories, be forced to admit that his contribution to the world situation has been incidental. For he insisted that it is not the ideas of anyone which produces world movements and change but simply the development of the modes of production.

This man, who lived to declare that he was not a Marxist,[3] is the most controversial figure to arise out of the nineteenth century to disturb the peace of the twentieth. As Paul Tillich warns, "His name has become so potent a political and semi-religious symbol, divine or demonic, that whatever you say about him will be used against you by fanatics on both sides."[4] We cannot help comparing him with Jesus Christ, who has disturbed not one but twenty centuries and whose followers are today opposing those of Marx.

THE PURPOSE OF THIS STUDY

There is no better point which one can choose to compare Christianity and Communism than their interpretations of history. The doctrine of history is essential to both. This is clear in Communism, which interprets the path history has followed, where it is going, and how it will get there. The society of the future, the Communist Party, the political aims,

[3] Franz Mehring, *Karl Marx*, tr. Edward Fitzgerald (New York: Covici Friede, 1935), p. 553.
[4] "How Much Truth Is There in Karl Marx?" *Christian Century*, Sept. 8, 1948, p. 906.

all depend upon an interpretation of history which gives the Communist hope and incentive.

At first sight it is not as apparent that Christianity is primarily a view of history. Christianity has frequently been distorted into a mystical or even mystery religion of individual salvation which denies or ignores the value of history in the sense of man's social life on earth. The prophetic Old Testament faith, however, upon which the New Testament built, was a religion which took history with utmost seriousness as the place of God's action and revelation. The New Testament, with its doctrine of the incarnation of God in a historical figure and the message of the coming Kingdom, obviously gives history a place of crucial importance.

Although Christianity is a history-affirming religion, it is at complete odds with the Marxian view that history can and will fulfill itself. If history is, to the Christian faith, the area of God's revelation and redemptive work, it is also the scene of man's rebellion. Thus all profound Christian views are eschatological. That is, they look beyond the present to find the final end and goal of man's history. The significance of the present depends upon the hope which the future holds. For the Christian this means that God's purposes for man are not limited to what can be achieved in this life or this world. As a result, the Christian cannot accept the present nature of history; it must be changed, redeemed by that which is beyond history.

It is often said that Communism is a religion. The late Archbishop William Temple called it a "Christian heresy." To make such statements raises a number of questions about terminology. There is no definition of religion that has satisfied all scholars. Various methods of definition have been employed. Sometimes religion has been defined in terms of cer-

tain beliefs. Such definitions usually describe religion as the belief in a supernatural being or in supernatural beings. Religion
has also been defined in terms of the psychological attitudes
of the religious man. One such definition has described religion as "ethics tinged with emotion."

For our purposes, I would like to make a tentative definition
of religion. I do not think that it is a perfect one, but it will
help to clarify what we mean when we speak of the religious
nature of Communism. From the point of view of belief we
may define religion as belief in a power or process, beyond
man, with which man can co-operate and which assures the
victory of good over evil. In this sense, Communism is a religion, for it believes that the process of dialectical materialism,
with which man can co-operate, is carrying man inevitably to
the victory of Communism. In terms of psychology, we will
use Paul Tillich's definition and say that a man is religious
when he is ultimately concerned and on the basis of this
concern makes an unconditional commitment. Certainly the
Communist is religious in this sense, for his concern with
Communism is ultimate; it takes precedence over all other
concerns; to it he says, "Not my will but thy will be done."
I hope that the full justification for calling Communism a
religion in this twofold sense will appear as we develop our
theme.

In referring to Communism as a religion, we must recognize the fact that Communists have never considered themselves religious. Defining religion in terms of belief in the supernatural and the afterlife, the Communists have attacked
all religion. Marx himself believed that religion was simply
an opiate to dull the pain of the oppressed so that they would
not demand their just rights. He charged that religion dis-
pels man's indignation at earthly injustice by promising him

that he will dwell in marble halls and walk the golden streets in the sweet by-and-by. Although Marx undoubtedly owed much of his passion for social justice to the Judaeo-Christian tradition which surrounded him, he made no exceptions in his blanket condemnation of religion. However, his close supporter and follower, Friedrich Engels, did see one religious group which won his praise—the German sectarian radicals who fomented the Peasants' Revolt in the sixteenth century. Engels expressed his admiration in his book *The Peasant War in Germany*.

Since the time of Engels several Communist-inspired writers have made sympathetic studies of various Christian sects. Today, in the Communist East Zone of Germany, the school children are being taught that the real hero of the Protestant Reformation was not Martin Luther but the revolutionary leader of the peasants, Thomas Münzer, a Christian sectarian. If we are to make a comparison of Christianity and Communism as religious interpretations of history, it is obvious that these Christian sects, which Communists admire, are a point of contact. But there is a deeper reason for looking at sectarian Christianity in this context. As we shall see, the full Christian message cannot be given without the witness of the sects.

I am using the term "sect" in the sense in which the German historian Ernst Troeltsch has made it famous in his monumental study, *The Social Teaching of the Christian Churches*.

The sect, according to Troeltsch, is that type of Christianity which arose from time to time to insist that the Christian had to be different from society, that the Church must include only the saints. The sect was shocked at the disparity between what the Church preached and what it often practiced. It was scandalized to see persons in the churches whose

lives showed no signs of Christian living. Sects believed that
the Church had broken faith with the New Testament by becoming assimilated to the world. Adult baptism was the symbol frequently used to represent their belief that one could
not enter the fold until he was mature enough to make a decision for Christ and to be a practicing Christian. This led
the sects to attack both Catholics and Protestants for having
become too much like the society in which they found themselves. Some sects believed that the world as a whole could not
achieve Christian perfection, so they withdrew from society,
but others felt called to redeem the whole social system.

The sects usually were drawn from the lower classes, the
proletariat of Marx, although leaders from other classes, particularly the clergy, were not wanting. The sects were critical
of a church which accepted the divisions of wealth and power
in the existing society. This meant that the sects criticized
the status quo in politics and economics in the name of a
higher Christian ethic.

The church (again following Troeltsch) is that form of
Christian organization which did not limit its membership to
the "saints." It recognized that the redeemed man is also a
sinner and did not believe that there could be a society of the
perfect. As a result, it did not try to withdraw from society,
but rather it remained in it, hoping that it could do more to
change society from within than it could by an exclusive withdrawal. The church hoped to include all the persons in a
given area, receiving them by baptism while they were infants.
This meant that the church was ever in danger of losing the
full Christian witness. It became so adjusted to the world
that it forgot that it was an outpost of heaven.

Because of the church's tendency to lose its full Christian
witness, it frequently needed to be jarred by a prophetic

voice, but often in its history it had no room within itself for such a voice. When this was the case, the prophetic message had to be expressed by a sect outside the church. The sect can be understood as an attempt to express Christian truths which a particular church had ignored. On the other hand, the sect seldom preached a balanced form of the gospel, since it was tempted to go to the opposite extreme from that of which it accused the church.

Because of this relation of church and sect, it is useful to think of the sect as the conscience of the church. When the church listened to its conscience, it was drawn from its complacent peace with the world. The church may have known that the sect had only a one-sided grasp of the Christian faith, but only at its own peril did the church forget that it was one side. Wherever the assimilation of the church to the world is criticized in the name of Jesus Christ, we have a sectarian tendency even if it does not produce a new Christian group. The great possibilities of the modern ecumenical movement include the possibility of bringing the sectarian and church types of thought together and thus preserving the values of both. Both are necessary if Christianity is to be complete.

Today, in America, it is obvious that none of our ecclesiastical institutions is a perfect example of either traditional type of organization. The church type, as Troeltsch describes it, is ideally a state-church, including all citizens of a political territory. This, of course, no longer exists in America. On the other hand, the so-called sects of modern America have, in many cases, lost all of the social radicalism that was traditionally associated with the sects. The modern American sects still emphasize the need to be different from the world, but only a few express this difference by trying to live the Sermon on the Mount, as did the Anabaptists and the early Quakers.

They are more likely to seek to be different by renouncing drinking, smoking, and dancing. Often they seek to be different by means of unusual spiritual experiences such as "speaking in tongues."

Furthermore, history shows that the longer a sect lived, the more it tended to take on the characteristics that Troeltsch finds in the church. As time passed, its members tended to be those who were born into it; it began to water down its differences from society and became respectable. It would seem that it is the destiny of a sect to become a church. Methodists, Baptists, and Quakers, all of whom began with sectarian tendencies, have come to adopt many aspects that Troeltsch identifies with the church.

Despite the fact that Troeltsch's types can seldom be found in their purity, the distinction is a useful one. It is useful to understand the history of Christianity, where certainly both types appear. Furthermore, it is relevant even today, as one finds within Christianity those who are inclusive and try to make the Church a part of society and those who are exclusive and wish to set the Church over against society. At the present time the sectarian tendency can express itself freely within most of our denominations, and it does not have to seek a separate organization, as was the case in the sixteenth and seventeenth centuries. This, no doubt, is one reason why the modern "sect" performs a function somewhat different from that which it performed in former times.

It would seem that both types of Christian thought are necessary to the welfare of organized Christianity. It is preferable that they both work in the same institution so that they can balance each other. Without the church attitude the Christians would become a clique, sorely tempted to self-righteousness. Without the sectarian emphasis the Christian witness would become watered down until Christian churches were nothing more than clubs, indistinguishable from the rest of society.

All of this may lead to a serious confusion in our use of words. The word "Church" has a twofold meaning in our terminology. In the first place, the Church means the universal society of men and women who have accepted Christianity and have become bound together into an organization. In this sense, of course, a sect is part of the Church, and sects have often claimed that they were the true Church. A few sects have substituted some word such as "meeting" for "church," but most sectarians would say that they "go to church." But, following Troeltsch, there is a technical meaning of "church" as opposed to sect. To avoid confusion, wherever the reference is to the "Church universal," it is capitalized. Wherever the reference is to the technical use of church as against sect, it is left uncapitalized.

Modern theology has been characterized by the rebirth of more orthodox thinking. This is not only true of those theologians who have been given the paradoxical title of "neo-orthodox," but it is true of almost all theological thinkers. The position of historic orthodoxy is held in much higher esteem on all sides than it was twenty or thirty years ago. Even the liberal theologians have realized that there are values in the historic tradition that were overlooked in the early days of liberalism. This new appreciation of orthodoxy has arisen, in part, from the fact that Christians have been confronted with the challenge of militant Communism.

When theologians such as Reinhold Niebuhr, Paul Tillich, Emil Brunner, and Karl Barth began to search Christian doctrine for an alternative to Communism, they found a new relevance in the thought of Paul, Augustine, Luther, and

Calvin. This, I believe, was a notable contribution to the richness and depth of Christian theology. Nonetheless, in facing the threat of Communism we need to pay more attention than has yet been paid to the sectarian tradition. George Fox, Gerard Winstanley, Menno Simons, and Joachim of Floris also have a word of prophecy to speak to our age. In other words, neo-orthodoxy needs to be balanced by a neo-heterodoxy. If this study seems to give an undue importance to the sectarians, it is because I feel that they have been neglected by Christians while their witness has been exploited by the Communists. Seen in their proper perspective, the sects are, I believe, a part of the Christian answer to Communism.

I CHRISTIAN AND COMMUNIST INTERPRETATIONS OF HISTORY

HISTORY, as we shall use the term, is not just a series or progression of events. History begins, as Augustine points out, with man's ability to transcend time. Man can, in a very real sense, transcend the present moment and look to the past with memory and to the future with anticipation. History is man's social life as it is remembered, comprehended, and anticipated. The philosophy of history is the attempt to find some pattern or meaning in the flow of remembered events so that one can understand the present and adjust himself to the future. By his philosophy of history a man decides for what he may hope and strive. By it he understands whence he came and whither he goes. Without a philosophy of history, man's life becomes a flux of meaningless events from which he may reap joy or sorrow but which cannot be seen within the framework of some wider meaning and purpose. The catastrophic nature of the twentieth century has produced a new interest in forming such a philosophy. What meaning can we discern in the chaotic events that surround us? Are they so much sound and fury, or are they but steps to a fuller and wider meaning of life?

It is improper to speak of *the* Christian philosophy or interpretation of history. Although there are certain common themes which run through the thinking of Christians upon this subject, there have been wide variations. We do not have the time to outline all such variations, but we will try to do justice to some of the more central interpretations.

THE BIBLE

The Bible is a book that takes history with great seriousness. This becomes particularly evident if we compare it with the literature of religions and philosophies which have seen no meaning in history. The Bible finds the revelation of God in history, whereas other religions have often sought salvation by flight into mystic absorption out of history or in an after-life. Against this the Bible teaches that salvation comes within history and that history itself is to be redeemed.

Many views of history, including those of some Greek philosophers, pictured history as going around in circles and repeating itself without anything qualitatively new occurring. The true meaning of life, therefore, had to be found outside the realm of history in some form of heaven where the personality of the individual might or might not be preserved. Against this the Bible presents a history that some have described as a straight line; that is, a history that has a beginning and an end, that is going some place and into which the qualitatively new can come.

The Bible begins with God's creation of the world, which is good. Creation makes it evident that God has a purpose for man. Yet the purpose of creation is in God. That is, creation is not an end in itself. The meaning of history depends upon that which is outside or beyond history. History is under the lordship of God.

From the Old Testament it becomes evident that history is moving to an end or goal. This end will fulfill the meaning of history, for it will overcome the vicissitudes of history which continually threaten its meaning. It is in history that

God reveals himself. He has not revealed himself in timeless principles whose truth would stand anywhere as self-evident; he reveals himself in the events of history. God's purpose for history, while no doubt beyond man's full comprehension, is partially revealed in God's choice of and covenant with the Jewish people, through whom the whole world is to be brought to God. Through this revelation the Jew learned that God, as the Lord of history, is in control of all the nations. He does not play favorites. If the Jew is chosen, it is for God's purpose and for the welfare of all men. To be chosen is a difficult burden to bear and one that brings with it particular obligations of service.

Although God is the Lord of history, the Old Testament finds that history does not progress inevitably. History is the scene of man's rebellion, symbolized in the defiance of God by Adam and Eve. History must be redeemed, changed. Man must be forgiven and restored to the relationship with God for which he was created. The faith that such redemption and forgiveness will occur is based not upon man's ingenuity or powers but entirely upon the nature of God. The Old Testament looks forward with hope to the coming age in which "the wolf also shall dwell with the lamb, and the leopard shall lie down with the kid; and the calf and the young lion and the fatling together; and a little child shall lead them" (Isa. 11:6). In this hope history is not to be denied; it is to be fulfilled. The historical forms, animals and men, are there, but the disharmonies are overcome. This final fulfillment of history gives to the Old Testament its hope, and it gives a meaning to the present life, no matter how painful or undesirable it may be.

The New Testament continues this theme. Again in history there occurs the event which reveals God—the coming of the

Messiah, Jesus Christ. In Christ, the New Testament finds
the meaning of history revealed. Jesus preached the hope of
the coming judgment in which God's sovereignty would be
revealed, the wicked overcome and punished, and the good re-
ceived into eternal fellowship with God.

Modern scholars have debated at great length about the
meaning of the Final Judgment or the apocalyptic Second
Coming of Christ in the teachings of Jesus. Some have
claimed that Jesus taught that the kingdom of God was
purely future and would be ushered in by his apocalyptic return upon the clouds of heaven, after which he should overthrow all the forces of evil.[1] Others have argued that Jesus
taught a "realized eschatology"—that is, that the Kingdom
had already come with himself and his actions.[2] The only
way in which we can do justice to all the facts seems to be to
accept elements of both views.

In some sense, Jesus certainly taught that the Kingdom had
come and that men could enter into it in the present age.[3]
Likewise Paul taught that it was possible for men to be de-
livered from the evil age even now (Gal. 1:4). The disciples
found in Jesus the assurance that God had entered decisively
into history, illustrated particularly by the miracles with which
Jesus overcame the forces of evil (Luke 11:20). The resurrection of Jesus was seen as the assurance that the first fruits of
the age-to-come had appeared. In some sense, then, the kingdom of God was already here as a result of the coming of
Christ. Henceforth history could be dated B.C. and A.D., for

[1] See Albert Schweitzer, The Quest of the Historical Jesus (New York:
The Macmillan Co., 1948).
[2] See C. H. Dodd, The Parables of the Kingdom (London: Nisbet &
Co., 1935).
[3] See Matt. 13:31-33, 44-45; 20:1-16; Mark 4:26; 12:34; and Luke 7:28;
17:20-21.

the event which revealed the meaning of all history had occurred.

On the other hand, there is no doubt that there is a sense in which Jesus teaches that the Kingdom is still to come; it was promised, rather than fulfilled, by Jesus' first appearance. Jesus looked forward to the final judgment and the final victory of good over evil (Mark 13; Luke 21:27-28). In other words, while the Kingdom was in some sense present with Jesus, it was present in a hidden form. Jesus had revealed the kingship of God, but it was revealed only to those who had eyes to see. The time was to come when the eyes of the blind would be opened and the kingship of God would no longer be hidden. The Kingdom which had come in promise with Jesus was to come with power. The decisive battle with evil had been fought and won by Jesus, but history continued. Although defeated, evil still had sufficient strength to fight a stubborn rear-guard action.

The early Christians apparently had high hopes that the Second Coming was to occur in the near future. This did not mean that they ignored the present; rather they turned to it with renewed activity because they had hope for the future. As time passed, however, there was an increasing tendency to think of the Second Coming in the more distant future. The concept of eternal life begins to replace the apocalyptic coming as the hope of the Christians. This is evident in the Gospel of John, written later than the other three Gospels. Even here, there is a present and a future element. Eternal life, as the Kingdom in the other Gospels, can be entered here and now; it is not just life beyond the grave (John 6:54; 17:3; I John 3:14-15; 5:11-12). On the other hand, it is also the future life with God beyond and after death (John 10:28; 12:25; I John 2:24-25).

THE AUGUSTINIAN OR ORTHODOX INTERPRETATION

One of the earliest and still one of the greatest attempts to formulate a complete philosophy of history was that of Augustine. While the Roman Empire was falling before the successive blows of the barbarian hordes, Augustine spent thirteen years, from 413 to 426, in writing his epic book, *The City of God*. In the first place, he was concerned with answering the charge of many Romans that the fall of the Empire was due to the rise of Christianity and the neglect of the gods who had made Rome powerful. In order to answer this charge he found it necessary to develop a complete philosophy of history.

Basic to Augustine's theory was the belief that there are two cities or societies, the City of God and the City of the World. The City of God includes the good angels and the righteous men upon earth. The City of the World contains the fallen angels and wicked human beings. The City of God is characterized by the selfless love of God, while the other city is formed upon the basis of immoderate self-love.

Time, and thus history, begins with the creation of the universe. After creation, some of the created angels rebelled, in the pride of their self-love, and thus was born the City of the World. Although the wills of these angels were evil, God has the power to use even this rebellion for his own purposes.[4] Thus Augustine lays the theological foundation for the relation between the two cities upon earth. Despite the fact that all the political states belong to the earthly city, they are useful to God.

Augustine declares that God's providence remains in control of the nations even when they refuse to acknowledge him.

[4] Augustine *The City of God* XI. 17.

The true reason for the long success of Rome was not that Jove had helped it; it was that God had ordained that it should be so. Consequently, Augustine goes to great lengths to refute the contemporary theories that fate rules the destinies of the nations. Against those Greek views which saw history going around in circles and repeating itself, Augustine asserts that history, under God, has a purpose and a goal.

Among the nations of the world, God chose the Jewish nation that within it there might be built the City of God. There were other individuals, among the other nations, who also belonged to the heavenly city, just as some Jewish individuals failed to belong to it. But no other people were chosen as a group. Finally, in the one man Jesus Christ, God himself appeared to make manifest the purpose and meaning of the whole of history. Jesus founded the Church, which was henceforth to embody the City of God upon earth. Thus, in the time of his writing, Augustine found that the City of God was represented by the Church, while the City of the World was represented by the Roman Empire.

The Church was not identical with the City of God. Not all members of the Catholic Church were members of the celestial city. In fact, not all members could even hope for salvation.[5] On the other hand, while the Roman Empire was essentially evil, it did perform certain real services for the Church in its maintenance of a certain amount of peace and concord. Although its reasons for seeking this peace were purely prudential and selfish, and rather like those that led to honor among thieves, the Church could still profit from it to spread its gospel. As a result, the Christian must pray for

[5] *Ibid.* XXI. 25.

the state, fight for it when its wars were just, and accept positions of authority within it. This is possible because, so long as this world exists, there will be an overlapping of interest between the two cities in the orderly maintenance of mortal life. This harmony, however, cannot be complete, for the laws of religion will not be the same for both cities.[6] At this point the heavenly city will have to dissent from the state, and it both has suffered and will suffer for doing so.

The fall of the Roman Empire was not, insists Augustine, due to its betrayal of its national gods. It was due rather to the nature of all states which bear within themselves the seeds of destruction. The Roman people were bound together as a people by their love of common objectives. As time passed, these objectives became less and less ideal. Self-love became more excessive and imperialistic. The people rose up against one another in civil strife, and thus was broken the concord which is the minimum necessity to hold together an earthly state. Rome fell because of her sin, not because of disaffection from her gods.[7]

What is the goal to which the historical process is moving? Augustine denied the view which we know as premillennial. This view is based upon a literal reading of the book of Revelation and holds that the Devil is to be chained for a thousand years after the coming of Christ, during which time there will be perfect peace upon earth for the saints, who will reign with God. At the close of the thousand years the Devil will be loosed, and there will follow the cataclysmic battle between Christ and the Antichrist, when even the saints will be sorely tried and some will fall. Finally, after his victory, Christ will judge the living and the resurrected dead; the present earth

[6] *Ibid.* XIX. 17.
[7] *Ibid.* XIX. 24.

will be transmuted into the heavenly kingdom of eternity. Augustine comments that although he had once held this view, he came to see it as too materialistic and based upon a faulty reading of the Scriptures.

Augustine insists that the "first resurrection" is not the resurrection preceding the thousand years of the millennium, but rather it is the resurrection of the soul that has been dead in sin and trespasses. Consequently, the first resurrection occurred with the coming of Christ. The "thousand years" began with Christ and is not to be taken literally as meaning a thousand years, but "thousand" is the perfect number and is symbolic of the perfect nature of God's kingdom. The kingdom of God has thus come and is present in the Church despite the fact that the Church is to be purified, at the Final Judgment, of the tares that now grow within it. When the Last Judgment comes and the second resurrection occurs, history will be ended, and the righteous will be transmuted to heaven to enjoy the perfect peace of fellowship with God, while the unrighteous will be condemned for eternity. In short, the final stage of history is present, and man cannot hope for a perfect earthly society in the future.

Augustine finds meaning in the whole of history. This meaning is dependent upon the goal toward which history is moving, a goal which lies outside history. In fact, Augustine takes pains to point out the absurdity and hopelessness of those who would find the meaning and purpose of history within history, or within this earthly life.[8] On the other hand, the goal is the fulfillment of history and does not simply deny it. Within history are fought the battles between good and evil; within history man makes his choice as to which city he shall join. The goal is thus more than history, but it includes history and does not ignore it.

For a thousand years or more Augustine was the reigning influence in the Christian interpretation of history. His theory of the two cities was the doctrinal basis for the relentless battle of the Middle Ages between secular rulers and the pope. The degree to which Augustine had identified the Church with the kingdom of God was used by the popes as the basis of their claims to supremacy over secular rulers. At the same time, the sharp distinction that Augustine had made between membership in the visible Church and membership in the City of God, or invisible Church, was neglected or forgotten. It became increasingly difficult for the Church to see itself under the judgment of God. Rather it felt that it was expressing the judgment of God upon the states of this world. Where Augustine had little hope that the two cities could co-operate on laws concerning religion, the Church increasingly sought to have the state enforce its religious laws, including religious orthodoxy.

In making his break with Roman Catholicism, Martin Luther relied at many points upon Augustine. This was true of his view of history. Like Augustine, Luther saw two cities, which he called the Kingdom of God and the Kingdom of the World. These cities were in continual conflict with each other. He was more careful than Augustine to avoid identifying either kingdom with any existing institution. The Church, with many unchristian men and imperfect Christians, did not fulfill the will of God completely. On the other hand the Kingdom of the World represented what man's life would be like if it were not restrained by the state's law. Thus, neither kingdom was in actual existence; the conflict between them divided both Church and state down the middle.

Luther was certain that the perfect society could not appear upon earth. He criticized those Anabaptists who thought that the state could be made Christian. The very nature of the state is coercion, declares Luther, while that of the gospel is persuasion. The state is a necessity provided by God because of the sin of man and hence is of value to God and the Church because it maintains order. But the state is not divine and may not become totalitarian, for the soul and spirit of man and the Church itself must be free to obey God rather than man. Luther counseled resistance to the state if it forces one to act in an unchristian manner, but he rejected rebellion.

If the prince of a state is a Christian, he ought to do all in his power to advance Christianity, believed Luther. This is not, however, to include persecution of heretics for heretical beliefs.[9] Luther did call the princes to suppress the Peasants' Revolt, but the peasants were to be suppressed as revolutionaries, not as heretics. Before the revolt, Luther had advised the princes to concede some of the peasants' demands and had advised the peasants not to revolt. Luther had a great fear of anarchy which lead him to sanction injustice if the only alternative was revolution.

Luther did not believe in any form of theocracy. One of his chief arguments against the Roman Catholic Church was that it had absolutized a human institution, the Church, and had tried to enforce the rule of the Church over all men with the aid of the state. When the Anabaptists tried to set up the theocratic rule of the saints, Luther opposed it as forcibly as he had opposed the papal rule and for the same reasons.

[9] Roland Bainton, *Here I Stand* (New York and Nashville: Abingdon Press, 1950), pp. 262, 314.

Nonetheless, Luther did not believe in a complete separation of Church and state. The two could and must cooperate with each other as fellow servants of God. This was no doubt dangerous to the purity of the Church, but Luther believed that it was a risk that the Church must take for the greater good of mankind.

Calvin also remained essentially within the Augustinian view of history. He considered that premillenarianism was too absurd to require a refutation upon his part.[10] The perfect kingdom, which will be without government, is a spiritual kingdom of the afterlife and will not be attained upon this earth, where sin will make civil government necessary to the end.

Calvin took a more positive view of the state than did either Augustine or Luther. He believed that government was a gift of God for the welfare of man. It had a positive duty to aid man to live the good life as well as to restrain evil. It ought to enforce religious laws as well as civil ones, and this meant, in practice, the political suppression of heresy.[11]

Calvin was sympathetic to a theocracy, ruled by the laws of the Bible. In agreement with Augustine and Luther, Calvin believed that God's providence ruled over history so that even the acts of evil men were used for the greater glory and purpose of God. At this point, Calvin's predestinarian concepts strengthened his conviction that all events were under God's sovereignty. Calvin was closer than Luther to the sectarian view of the Church. Where Luther found the marks of the true Church in faith and sacraments, Calvin looked for "discipline" in addition to these. That is, Calvin sought to make the visible Church into a society of practicing Christians.

[10] John Calvin, *Institutes of the Christian Religion*, III, xxv, 5.
[11] *Ibid*, IV, xx, 3 and 9.

THE SECTARIAN INTERPRETATION OF HISTORY

The Augustinian interpretation of history was challenged by the sectarian. The first Christian sect was that of Montanism, which began under the leadership of Montanus about the year 156. Montanism criticized the church of its day for having lost the rigor of the early church. It revived the belief that the apocalypse, or Second Coming of Christ, was imminent in time, and it called the saints apart from society to prepare for the end. It also criticized the idea that revelation was past and insisted that the Holy Spirit could still speak to men as it had spoken to them in the past. This sect, although limited in numbers, continued for some two or three centuries.

After Augustine, there was no serious threat to the dominance of his interpretation of history until it was challenged by Joachim of Floris (d. 1202). Joachim was a strange figure, a Cistercian abbot, who appealed greatly to the left-wing followers of Francis of Assisi. Augustine, as we have seen, placed the thousand years of Christ's rule in the present and found it manifested in the Church. Joachim challenged this by claiming that the thousand years lay in the future. This meant that the contemporary Church situation was neither the kingdom of God upon earth nor final.

Joachim used the Trinity to interpret history. He saw three stages in history, corresponding to each of the Persons of the Trinity. The age of the Father, beginning with Adam and continuing until the birth of Christ, was the age of the law. During it marriage was the rule, and even polygamy was sanctioned. Private property, wealth, and the carnal life in general were all taken for granted and even extolled. During the age of the Son, which began in the reign of Uzziah, although it did not come to power until the time of Christ, there was a real advance over the old age. Polygamy was replaced by monogamy. The law was replaced by the free relationship to God which is known as grace. It was the age in which the Church was ruled by the priests. In short, whereas the first age was a carnal age, the second was a mixture of flesh and spirit.

The third age, that of the Spirit, had begun with the rule of Benedict in the fifth century, but it was still to come in full power in the year of 1260. It would be ushered in, Joachim forecast, with an attack upon Christendom by the Mohammedans. The new age would be an age of pure spirituality. Marriage would be replaced by celibacy, and the celibate saints would live forever. Poverty and the renunciation of private property would be the marks of the spiritual man. Love, liberty, peace, and joy would abound upon earth. Since the kingdom of God and the state are incompatible, there would be no governmental rule or political power to mar the future age of perfection. The Church itself would no longer be ruled by the hierarchy but by the Spirit of God speaking in the hearts of the individual Christians.

Although there was much in Joachim that seems esoteric to us, he is important because he challenged the Augustinian idea that the kingdom of God is present and that therefore man cannot look forward to a better age in the future. Joachim taught that each of the three ages is more perfect than that which preceded it. In keeping with this he subjected the *status quo* of both Church and state to radical judgment. In particular, Joachim considered that the wealth and political power of the Church were incompatible with the will of God.

There is for Joachim, however, no smooth progress from one age to the next. Rather there are suffering, conflict, and testing. The new age arises out of the death agonies of the old. One cannot help seeing broad similarities to Communism in the thought of this medieval heretic. Communism also sees stages in history, beginning "within the womb" of the old, coming to birth in revolution and crisis, and finally bringing forth the age of perfect brotherhood and renunciation of private property.

The actual followers of Joachim were few in number and formed a heretical fringe of the church of the Middle Ages. They tended to disintegrate after 1260, when Joachim's forecasts failed to materialize. Joachim, however, was read by later sectarians such as Thomas Münzer who did not follow his thought in detail but who did look to the future for the kingdom of God.

Sectarianism found its fullest expression in the Protestant Reformation. We are particularly interested in the continental Anabaptist groups and the English sects of the Cromwellian period, for it is with these that Communist writers have found common ground. Actually, there were a large number of these sects, and, as they varied considerably, we can only summarize certain basic trends among them.

An objective study of the Reformation sects was long delayed because they left few records. We know about them from what their enemies had to say of them. For example, David Russen, writing in the eighteenth century of Anabaptist influences in England, charges them with every conceivable heresy, including Apollinarianism, Marcionism, Novationism, Donatism, Catharism, and Pelagianism; then, for good measure, he charges that they are sponsored by the

Jesuits.[12] Such interpretations were accepted as quite objective until the twentieth century.

Toward the end of the nineteenth century a truer picture began to appear. The Christian pioneer in this field was Richard Heath, who began to dig beneath the countless misconceptions and false charges to write a very fair history of these groups.[13] About the same time a rabid defense of the sects came from Communist sources. Engels himself wrote glowingly of the Anabaptists' forerunners who were responsible for the Peasants' War.[14] Belfort Bax contributed two volumes and Karl Kautsky another to glorify and defend the Anabaptists.[15] The English sects were treated by Eduard Bernstein and others.[16] These writings have a special interest for our study. They reveal the extent to which Communists have detected parallels between themselves and the sects. We would be making a serious mistake, however, to suppose that the parallels are as close as these writers make them appear to be. We must counterbalance their view with that of modern Baptists, Quakers, and Mennonites, several of whom have rediscovered their glorious ancestors.

The net result of these researches, Marxian and Christian, has been to give us a new clue to the nature of the sects. They

[12] *Fundamentals Without Foundation, or a True Picture of the Anabaptists* (London, 1703), pp. 70-75.

[13] *Anabaptism: From Its Rise at Zwickaw to Its Fall at Munster* (London, 1895).

[14] Friedrich Engels, *The Peasants War in Germany*, tr. M. J. Olgin (New York: International Publishers, 1926).

[15] Belfort Bax, *The Peasants War in Germany* (London and New York, 1899), *Rise and Fall of the Anabaptists* (London and New York, 1903). Karl Kautsky, *Communism in Central Europe in the Time of the Reformation*, tr. J. L. and E. G. Mulliken (London, 1897).

[16] Eduard Bernstein, *Cromwell and Communism*, tr. H. J. Stemning (London: George Allen & Unwin, Ltd., 1930).

are no longer seen as a fanatical perversion of the true Reformation; rather they are recognized, in many ways, as the ones who carried the Reformation to its logical conclusions and as a sincere expression of certain valid aspects of the Christian faith.

The Communists' interest in these groups is justified by the fact that in each case the sectarian religious protest was aimed at social evils, political and economic, as well as at ecclesiastical ills. Beginning in the fifteenth century, there had been a series of semireligious rebellions in Germany. The peasants were conscious of exploitation and injustice and appealed to religious ideals to justify their rebellion. These revolts were sometimes Catholic and sometimes anti-Catholic, but the discontent that they expressed was favorable to the Protestant Reformation. The Reformation, however, did not bring the rapid social changes for which the peasants hoped; and when, taking things into their own hands, they revolted, Luther turned against them. Henceforth they were ripe for the Anabaptist harvest.

The Peasants' War found a leader in the radical sectarian Thomas Münzer. He had once been a follower of Luther, but he had become disillusioned with what he considered Luther's conservatism. He accused Luther of preaching the forgiveness of Christ too exclusively and forgetting that Christ also called men to take up their cross. Münzer believed that Christians must overthrow the evil society and set up a Christian socialism in its place. The Peasants' Revolt, under his leadership, was crushed with great ferocity.

Later, in 1532, the Anabaptists took over the city of Munster, in which their prophets had foretold they were destined to set up the kingdom of God. An attempt was made to build a communistic-Christian society, and Anabaptists flocked to the city from all over Europe. The Bishop of Munster raised an army, besieged the city, and finally subdued it amidst great cruelty.

After the fall of Munster the fighting Anabaptists were discredited, and the pacifist groups came to the fore. In due time Menno Simons became the recognized leader of the Anabaptists. He preached a philosophy of Christian pacifism and sectarian withdrawal from the world.

The Mennonites had no more love for the *status quo* or the state than their fighting brethren. They refused to hold political office or to protect the state, but, as pacifists, they had no patience with revolution. In fact, they did not even attempt to change society by peaceful methods. The Mennonites fled from society to practice their Christianity in small, often semicommunist groups. The coming of the Kingdom was left completely to God. In the interval before the end, the community of saints prepared themselves for its coming.

The followers of Menno Simons met with violent persecution and abuse, being charged with crimes similar to those attributed to the people at Munster. Nevertheless, the group persevered and still is an active force in the world today.

The sectarian groups flourished in England during and following the Civil War (1642-49). Under Cromwell, the Republican army became an army of religious enthusiasts, drawn together by a mutual hate of episcopacy and autocratic rule. After the revolution was successful, the groups which had joined in their opposition to the king were sharply divided over what to put into his place. One group was Presbyterian and longed to see a Presbyterian church made the state church of England as it was of Scotland. This group had little conception of giving liberty to dissenters from its viewpoints. Socially it was bound up with the more wealthy classes of the revolution and was strictly conservative. It was not opposed to monarchy as such and would gladly have restored it under suitable checks upon its power. It was definitely opposed to anything that questioned the sanctity of private property or the economic *status quo*. Independents or Congregationalists formed the second group. This group was more sympathetic to the claims of toleration but was conservative on economic questions. It was suspicious of the power of Parliament and of Presbyterianism. The third group consisted of several left-wing sects. Socially they represented the poorer classes, although they had many spokesmen from upper classes. For the most part, they stood for a complete freedom of religion. Large elements of them held radical social and political ideas.

Among the more important English sects were the Levellers, the Diggers, the Fifth Monarchy men, and the Quakers. The Levellers, led by John Lilburne and William Walwyn, believed that God was the supreme ruler of the universe. As a consequence they fought all arbitrary or authoritarian rule of man over man. They wanted a democratic England, free from a state church.

The Diggers broke away from the Levellers. Believing in the sinfulness of private property, they began to dig the Commons at Cobham in 1649 as a symbol of the right of all men to work the land. Although they never grew to significant numbers, their leader, Gerard Winstanley, was a rare genius whose works have been rediscovered in recent years.

The Fifth Monarchy men believed that the fifth and final monarchy, the rule of Christ upon earth, was about to come. This was based upon the four beasts of the book of Daniel, which were believed to be the four empires of Babylon, Persia, Greece, and Rome. The fourth, or Roman, monarchy was falling with the rule of the pope, and so the monarchy of Christ would soon come. One group of Fifth Monarchy men was pacifist and waited for Christ to send the Kingdom. But another group was revolutionary and twice revolted under Thomas Venner, believing that it was their duty, as the saints, to help God in bringing in his Kingdom.

The Quakers were pacifists who believed that the Inner Light or Spirit of God spoke to every man. Under the leadership of George Fox, the group repudiated the ecclesiastical and social customs of their time. They held their society under the radical judgment of Christ's teaching and found it wanting.

During the Civil War there was a widespread feeling that this was the war of the "last times," that the forces of the Lord, the Republicans, were locked in the last titanic struggle with the forces of evil, the Monarchists. Men felt that they were on the threshold of the kingdom of God, in which their injustices—economic, political, and religious—were to be wiped out. The inevitable result of such hopes was a widespread disillusionment. As soon as the victory was gained, it became evident that the many hopes were not to be fulfilled. The sects, where apocalyptic hopes had been strongest, were particularly disillusioned, as Cromwell's victory brought neither religious freedom nor economic amelioration. Throughout the sectarian literature of this period there runs a note of disillusioned protest. Despite this disillusionment, however, the hope did not die out, for an apocalyptic hope is of such a nature that it is likely to be strengthened by tribulations. When the saints suffer, it represents the last persecutions, which herald the coming of the Kingdom (Mark 13:14-23). The sects became convinced that the God who had enabled them to overthrow the bishop and the king would soon overthrow the presbyter and Parliament, which were too often taking the place of the former tyranny.

This quick summary of the sects will reveal something of their diversity. It cannot be expected that they would have a completely unified interpretation of history, although certain features do appear to be common among them. Let us summarize some of the main points that were held by most or all of the sects.

The sects were united in believing that the Church ought to consist of saints only. A saint did not mean to the sects a man who withdrew to a monastery; a saint was a man who, in the fullness of his maturity, had made a decision to follow and obey Christ. The sect was to be the outpost of the kingdom of God, living the Christian life as if the Kingdom were already here.

As a symbol of their belief, most of the sects insisted upon adult baptism. This was not because baptism was so important; they actually put little stock in the sacraments except as signs of an inner grace. In fact, the Quakers repudiated all outward sacraments. But when the adult submitted to baptism, he symbolized his mature choice of Christianity. Infant baptism meant that persons were taken into the Church who had not dedicated themselves to the living of the Christian life. In fact, the practice of gaining members through infant baptism was seen as one of the prime reasons for the failure of the Church to be radically Christian. Furthermore, the sectarians believed in a return to primitive or New Testament Christianity, and they found no sanction for infant baptism there.

With the emphasis upon the need to return to primitive Christianity, there went particular concern with the ethical teachings of Jesus. They denied that any man could be considered a Christian who did not obey the Sermon on the Mount. This tended to make them suspicious of the Protestant doctrine of salvation by grace alone. Although they recognized the need for divine forgiveness, they were afraid that the Protestant doctrine of salvation would lead to unreformed lives in the Reformed Churches. Nothing must hide the fact that the Christian was meant to be one who was different from the world.

Since they called Christians to return to the primitive Church, they believed that there had been a falling away from the original purity of the faith. Some dated this fall from the time of Constantine, when Christianity became a state-supported religion. Others felt that it came at the close of the New Testament period. At any rate, they believed that Church history had been the history of growing apostasy. Christianity must be thoroughly purged. The Protestant Reformation, they admitted, had made a good start in overthrowing the papacy, indulgences, and other Catholic practices. But it had stopped too soon, they felt. It had kept many of the evil accretions of the centuries, such as infant baptism. The sects called for "Reformation without Tarrying."

In their radical demand that the Church be purified, the sects had little hope for aid from the state. In fact, most of them were completely antagonistic to the state. Some, as we have seen, actually revolted against the existing governments, but even the pacifist groups refused to co-operate in any way with the state. The sectarian would not take oaths, serve in official state churches, or fight in the armies. Among the sects was born the demand for a separation of Church and state, and by the sectarian Roger Williams this ideal was brought to the United States, where it was to find its way into the Constitution. The sects, however, were somewhat divided at this point. Some of them hoped for the saints to take over the state and make it Christian. This was particularly true of the revolutionary Anabaptists and Fifth Monarchy men.

The sects looked upon the existing order of the world as basically evil. In particular, they railed against the state churches which raised worldly ecclesiastics to power and wealth. Against the state church the sects insisted upon the right of the individual to interpret the Bible for himself. This varied among the sects from a legalistic and literal interpretation of the Bible to a belief in the continuance of revelation which might supplant or contradict the Bible. For the same reason they insisted upon the right of laymen to preach; this was one of their chief scandals in the eyes of the official clergy.

The sectarian emphasis upon the evil nature of the world was not limited to the Church. It included also the injustices and inequalities of society. In a truly Christian brotherhood there would be, they insisted, no rich and no poor. When the sects attacked luxuries, it was not, in most cases, because of an ascetic belief that material goods or pleasures are wrong. It was because of the belief that it is wicked for one man to have plenty or overabundance while another is starving. A typical statement in this regard is that of George Fox the Younger, who speaks not only for the Quakers but for the sects in general when he says:

O! the Spirit of the Lord is grieved and pressed with the iniquities and whoredoms of this generation. O! the Waste and

Spoyl, that is made in the Lord's creatures, excess in apparel, excess in Diet, and deceitful Feastings and Banquettings; . . . and in the meantime, your own flesh, or them of the same blood . . . stand in your streets, crying for a piece of Bread, and many of your Lame and Blind and sick and others, both in prisons and other places are ready to famish.[17]

Again, one cannot miss the political implications involved in the Quaker refusal to recognize differences in social rank and cast. Their refusal to take off their hats in the presence of their "betters," their dogged use of "thee" and "thou," were not simply strange religious quirks. They were socially revolutionary in a quiet and yet effective manner. They aimed a criticism at the very heart of the medieval stratification of society. Each of the sects had some method of protesting against these inequalities, which they viewed as violations of the brotherhood of man and the fatherhood of God.

If the sectarian believed that the present age was deplorably evil, he also believed that the new age was about to dawn. A strong hope for the apocalyptic Second Coming was a feature of nearly every one of the sects. God, they believed, was about to set up his perfect society here upon earth in fulfillment of the scriptural promises. This apocalyptic hope was seen both in terms of judgment and in terms of promise. It would bring woes to the wicked but deliverance, peace, and justice to the righteous and oppressed. We have seen that the Reformation in Germany and the Cromwellian wars in England fanned the flames of this hope among the sectarians.

The sects were in disagreement over the practical implica-

[17] *A Collection of Several Books and Writings Given Forth by That Faithful Servant of God and His People, George Fox, the Younger* (London, 1665), pp. 148-49.

tions of the apocalyptic hope. For some it meant that the saints were to take up the sword and revolt. These men, like Thomas Münzer, were certain that if God saw his saints in military difficulties, he would come to their aid and subdue their enemies. If God has delayed in sending his Kingdom, perhaps, they reasoned, he is waiting for the saints to act, and what act could better show their faith than to revolt in his name? To others, this was blasphemy. God alone would bring in his Kingdom, in his own good time. Some of these, however, such as Winstanley and his Diggers, felt called to perform certain peaceful acts which would herald the coming of the Kingdom. Hence they began to dig and plant the common lands in their expression of the belief that the day of earthly injustice was hastening to its close. Still others felt that they must simply prepare themselves and wait for God to send his Kingdom. For example, the Mennonites withdrew into their little pacifist groups and prepared for the end with prayer, brotherly living, and watchful waiting. They all agreed, however, that the foremost duty of the sect in such a time was to preach the message of the coming Kingdom and to send out the call for repentance to all the wicked that they might be saved as brands from the burning even at the eleventh hour.

It is evident that this sectarian interpretation of history has some elements in common with that of Augustine. The sects agree with Augustine that God is the sovereign Lord of history and that he has a purpose for history which is to be fulfilled. They agree that man cannot, by himself, fulfill his own or the world's destiny. They look forward with faith to the final triumph of good over evil, in which God will be vindicated and the saints of all the ages will share.

The differences, however, are equally evident. The Augustinian view emphasizes those aspects of Scripture which point to the fact that the Kingdom has come already with Christ and is upon earth even now. In doing this, it tends to lose hope for any radical change in man's social or earthly life. The sectarian view tends to lose sight of the fact that the Kingdom has come with Christ and thus puts its emphasis upon the radical change which can be expected in the future. Since the Augustinian view does not hold too much hope for radical change, it is more inclined to make use of existing institutions—such as the state. The sectarian, filled with hope for the glorious future, takes a more negative view of the institutions of the *status quo* and impatiently looks for a complete renewal or destruction of these institutions. For the sect, the City of God does not need and may not use the City of the World. It would be an oversimplification to say that the Augustinian view is conservative and the sectarian radical, but it is true that this is what they often have meant in practice.

The Christian sects were forerunners and pioneers of modern democracy. I cannot take the time here to justify this statement, but it has been amply demonstrated in several studies.[18] This is not to ignore the contribution that was made to democracy by the church type of Christian thought, particularly that of the Calvinists. But inasmuch as Communist

[18] See William Haller, *The Leveller Tracts, 1647-1653* (New York: Columbia University Press, 1944); *The Rise of Puritanism* (New York: Columbia University Press, 1938); *Tracts on Liberty in the Puritan Revolution, 1638-1647*, 3 vols. (New York: Columbia University Press, 1934). W. Schenk, *The Concern for Social Justice in the Puritan Revolution* (London; Longmans, Green & Co., 1948). A. S. P. Woodhouse, *Puritanism and Liberty* (London: J. M. Dent and Sons, Ltd., 1938).

writers have exploited the similarities between the sects and themselves, it is well that we keep in mind the democratic implications of sectarianism.

The sects led the battle for religious freedom. In the sixteenth and seventeenth centuries the key to freedom of thought was freedom of religion, as it probably still is. Even the forces of Cromwell were not unanimously in favor of such freedom. In those centuries most groups held the view that error has no rights; persecution is wicked only when it is used against the "truth." But among the Anabaptists and English sectarians there was the demand for freedom of thought, even the freedom to be wrong. Heretics were to be persuaded, they insisted, not forced into truth. This faith underlay their demand for the separation of Church and state. The American democracy was built, to a great extent, by the sectarians who came to this country.

The sectarians took the Protestant doctrine of the priesthood of all believers more seriously than any other Protestant group. They opened their pulpits to the tailors, shoemakers, and other "common people," thereby shocking the churchmen of their time. The priesthood of all believers meant to them the equality of all men before God, an equality that was to be respected by the state as well as by the Church.

The sects insisted that all authority came from the people and that the rulers must be subject to them.[19] They preached the desirability of universal suffrage centuries before any country adopted it.[20] They worked out, before John Locke, a social-contact theory of government.[21] By teachings and ac-

[19] See John Rogers, *Sagrir or Doomes-Day Drawing Nigh* (London, 1653), p. 120.

[20] See George Fox the Younger, *op. cit.*, p. 87.

[21] See John Lilburne, *Man's Free Worship Vindicated*, reprinted in Woodhouse, *op. cit.*; and W. Haller, *The Rise of Puritanism*, p. 368.

tions they made it clear that they did not believe that there was anything sacred about obedience to legal authorities if those authorities opposed the will of God or the conscience of his people. Typical of this attitude were letters written to Charles II, when he returned to his throne, by the two irrepressible Quakers, George Fox the Younger and James Naylor.[22] They reminded the King that his father had been dethroned and beheaded because he had failed God, and they warned that Charles would go the same way if he did not follow the will of God. As one marvels at the audacity of these letters to a king returning to the land that had rebelled against his father's rule, one recognizes the courage with which the sectarians laid the foundations of modern democracy.

It is well to keep this democratic contribution in mind. We are about to examine certain parallels between the sects and Communism; but, for all the similarities, it is apparent that there are decisive differences. The Communist theories have not yet been able to produce, in practice, anything but tyranny and oppression. Despite the sympathy which modern Communist writers have shown for the sects, the sectarians would, if alive today, oppose commissar and dictator as urgently as once they opposed bishop and king.

THE COMMUNIST INTERPRETATION OF HISTORY

The Communist interpretation of history is known as dialectical materialism. It is materialistic in the sense that it is opposed to all forms of idealism. It claims that ideas come from matter and not matter from ideas. In contrast to all Christian views, there is no room for a transcendent purpose

---

[22] George Fox the Younger, op. cit., pp. 93 ff. James Naylor, *A Collection of Sundry Books, Epistles and Papers* (London, 1716), p. 596.

which guides history and which is fulfilled beyond the bounds of space and time. There is, however, as we shall see, a force beyond man which is carrying him toward the goal which the Communists desire.

Communism teaches not simply materialism but dialectical materialism. Whereas other materialistic philosophies have been interested in describing the world, Marx was determined to change it, and dialectics was for him the science of change.[23] The world is seen by the Communists as being in continual change, which takes the form of conflict. Nature is an organically related whole in which phenomena are connected with, dependent on, and determined by one another. Because of the continuous change, the future always lies with the new and rising forces rather than with the old and established ones.[24] Change is not simply a gradual progress; it moves to a crisis in which the qualitatively new arises out of conflict with the old.

This dialectical process, which the Communist sees running through the whole of nature, is particularly significant in the historical life of man, where it gives rise to the concepts of economic determinism and class struggle. Economic determinism, or the economic interpretation of history, is an essentially simple concept. It is based upon the idea that before man can think or act, he must first live. To live he must eat, be clothed, housed, and so forth. The basic factor in life, therefore, is the search for the necessities of life. Every society has some mode of production whereby it produces the economic goods necessary for physical existence.

[23] See Marx and Engels, *The German Ideology*, edited with an Introduction by R. Pascal (New York: International Publishers, 1939), pp. 197, 199.
[24] See Joseph Stalin, *Dialectical and Historical Materialism* (New York: International Publishers, 1940), pp. 7-8.

Upon this mode of production rests all man's institutions, ideas, theories, laws, religion, philosophy, and ethics. When the means of production change, as they are continually doing, they force a change in all the other activities of man.

Economic determinism leads to class struggle. In any system of private property there is a division of the classes into those who have and those who do not have. The "haves" wish to retain the *status quo* which has blessed them with property, while the "have nots" wish for a change. The wish for change is powerless to bring it, and any moral or spiritual considerations are irrelevant. But when the mode of production changes, the dispossessed class has the power of history upon its side, so that it inevitably rises, while the former ruling class must pass from the scene. This change will not be made without conflict, for the rulers will fight to retain their privileges. Resistance, however, is useless for the laws of history are now with the rising class as once they were with the ruling class in its hour of triumph.

This enables us to understand the Communist boast that they have "scientific socialism." The "utopian" socialists, the Communists charge, preach socialism because they think that it is morally desirable. This preaching is so much sound and fury, for such appeals do not change society. The Marxian Communists, however, claim to make a scientific study of the laws of society and its change so that they can work with them.

Since man's thinking is dependent upon his economic substructure and since history is the continual scene of class struggle, Communists claim that all of man's thinking and his institutions are ultimately a defense of his class interest. The state is above all else the captive of class interest. It is the center of power which must be captured by the class that would rule. Democratic states are deplored as being nothing more than the tools of the capitalists, or "Wall Street," as contemporary Communist propaganda puts it.

History, the Communist believes, develops through a series of stages. It begins with the period of primitive communism. During this period life was simple; there was no private property of any consequence and hence no classes. The tribe or clan lived harmoniously, freely sharing the necessities of life without any of its members being exploited. Government and the enforcement of law were in the hands of the whole people, so that government was not, as in other stages, something apart from the people which could be used by one class to exploit other classes.

This early communism was destroyed as the means of production changed. Private property appeared, classes arose, and governments took on form apart from the people and fell into the hands of the property-owning class. This brought the period of slave economy. Slavery was now profitable, and human beings were bought and sold like animals.

A further change in means of production brought about the feudal economy. The new productive forces of this period required that the laborer should have some kind of initiative in production which slaves would not be likely to have. Consequently, there arose the class of serfs, men who were not owned by the landlord but who had to give the landlord free work in order that they might till the land for themselves.

With the industrial revolution and its new means of production, still another economic structure arose—capitalism. The factories and other means of production were owned by a few capitalists, and the wage earners worked for them. The capitalist paid back, in form of wages, only a part of what the laborer produced and kept for himself the remainder, called by Marx "surplus value." Since the wage earners did not earn enough to buy what they had produced, capitalism fell into depression and overproduction. Imperialism partially solved this by forcing colonial markets to take the surplus, but this was a limited field. An increasing competition among capitalists drove many to ruin, and control was concentrated into fewer and fewer hands. Since profits became more difficult to make, the capitalists had to exploit the workers more severely. Marx forecast that there would be an increasing misery of the proletariat because of this.

Beginning with this summary of the capitalist system, the Communists go on to forecast the future. Production has, they assert, become a co-operative and social affair, so that private property has lost its meaning. The proletariat, having been gathered into close-knit groups and trained to fight in imperialistic wars, will finally band under the Communist Party and revolt. Because the dialectics of history will be with them, they are certain to win. Capitalism thus bears the seeds of its own destruction.

When the proletariat wins its inevitable victory, it will set up the system known as the dictatorship of the proletariat. "Prehistory" will have ended, says Marx, and "history" will begin. That is, there is a qualitative difference separating the world after the revolution from that before it. This dictatorship is the transitional period between capitalism and communism, beyond which none of the existing communist societies claims to have gone. During this period the state will be taken over by the proletariat, and the last traces of capitalism will be destroyed. The economic system will be socialist, with the state owning the means of production. The goods produced are to be distributed in proportion to the amount of labor performed on the principle of "he who does not work, neither shall he eat." Exploitation will be, according to the theory, a thing of the past.

Finally, when all the remnants of capitalism have disappeared, the state will no longer be necessary, for the only purpose of the state is to enable the ruling class to suppress its opponents. When the proletariat has no more opponents, the state will naturally wither away for want of something to do. The proletariat will have no opponents because it is the class that will have become identical with the whole of the people. It is the destiny of the proletarian class to end all classes. Self-interest will no longer be the divisive force that it has been throughout history, for it will have nothing to work upon. The principle of distribution will be, "From each according to his ability, to each according to his need." With the rise of the proletariat, national differences will disappear, for the working class has no country. Consequently, wars will pass into oblivion along with class struggles and the state. History will now have arrived at the goal of complete perfection, and man will live happily and peacefully in co-operative fellowship with his fellow men.

Although the Communist system claims to be "scientific socialism" and denies that moral appeals can change society apart from changes in the mode of production, there is a great emphasis upon the ideals of justice. From the writings of Karl Marx to those of Joseph Stalin, there runs a passionate condemnation of exploiters and exploitation. Against these, the ideals of social equality and brotherly relations among men are extolled. The religious nature of Communism comes out when we see its faith that there are forces beyond man which assure the defeat of what it believes to be evil and the triumph of what it hails as good. Man does not have to struggle for his values in a universe that is unfriendly or indifferent to them. The meaning of life, for the Communist, is found in giving himself to these forces and working with them. Dialectical materialism does for the Communist what God does for the more traditional religions—it gives him the assurance that he is doing that which is right; it gives a meaning to his life and a hope for the future.

II A COMPARISON OF VIEWS

HAVING seen, in brief outline, the nature of Christian and Communist views of history, we are prepared to make some comparisons of them. In this chapter we are primarily interested in similarities between the two views. The radical differences between them will be brought out in later chapters. When we are looking for similarities, we find that we turn more often to the sects than to the Augustinian tradition. I believe that such a comparison will give substance to the belief that Communism is a religion and to Archbishop Temple's point that it is a "Christian heresy." The word "heresy" is to be applied, of course, in a poetic rather than in a technical sense. Communism is "Christian" only in the sense that it shares certain ideals of the Christian culture in which it grew. It is heretical in the sense that these ideals take on a perverted form within the Communist context.

THE GOLDEN AGE AND THE FALL

The first striking similarity between Christian and Communist views of history is that both begin with the thought of a golden age in the past and a fall therefrom.[1] For many centuries Christians thought of the Genesis story of Adam and Eve as a literal explanation of how evil and sin came into the world. Man had begun in idyllic perfection but had fallen before the sly temptation that he might become as God. At

[1] For a further discussion of these similarities see my article "The Relevance of the Fall" in *Religion in Life*, XX (Winter, 1951), pp. 99-105.

the present time there are many theologians who deny the historicity of the first three chapters of Genesis but who believe that the concept of a golden age and fall is extremely meaningful as a mythical presentation of man's condition.

For the Communists the golden age is represented by the primitive communism which they believe characterized the society of the earliest men. In this primitive state there was no private property, no government separate from the people as a whole, and no exploitation of one man by another. Engels gives us the clearest picture of this in his book *The Origin of the Family, Private Property and the State*. Into this peaceful and harmonious scene there came a change in the methods of production which led to private property. This, like the serpent in the Garden of Eden story, led to a host of ills and the fall of man. Man began to exploit his fellow men; government became class government, which ruled in the interests of part of the people instead of the whole. Even the sex relationship was perverted. Instead of being based upon natural love, as it had been under the early communism, it became chained to marriage for the purposes of property inheritance. Woman ceased to be the free and equal partner of man and became instead his property whose sole duty was to raise sons to inherit their father's wealth. Wars became more widespread and vicious. In short, the whole of man's life was corrupted almost beyond recognition.

Among the sectarians the idea of the past golden age took on an even greater importance than it has in the other forms of Christianity. The sects, almost invariably, believed that man is perfectible. This perfection was to be manifested in the coming kingdom of God and/or in the sect itself as a society apart from the world. All men, even the most radical, have a strong desire to stand with the past, or to appear as something more than a crank advocating a novel idea of a society that never was or will be. Therefore, if one can declare that his dreams are not spun from idle fancy but that once conditions were like this, the radical has robbed the conservative of the latter's strongest weapon—the argument that what never has been never can be. So the sectarian dwelt much on the glories of the Garden of Eden, and to strengthen his point, he pictured the glories and perfection of the primitive Church before it fell into its "Roman" corruptions. Continually the sects were attempting to get back to the New Testament period, when Christianity had been lived perfectly.

This emphasis upon past golden ages may seem out of place in essentially radical movements which are looking ahead. But it gives a greater faith for the future. To the Protestant who argued that original sin was too stubborn to be cast out and that all men, even the redeemed, remained sinners, the sectarians replied that Adam had been sinless and that Jesus, the Second Adam, had come to restore the possibilities that were the first Adam's before the Fall. When churchmen of all types declared that the Church could not be made up of the saints only but must include sinners and those weak in the faith, the sectarians responded that the New Testament Church had been a church of saints and that all churches were called to be like it. When the Catholic declared that his church was hallowed by centuries and went back to Christ himself, the sectarians countercharged that they, not the Catholics, really went back to the Church of Christ. Catholicism was a degeneration of the early Church, while the sect was a restoration of it.

Here we find Communist thought very similar to that of the sectarian. Why does Engels strive at such great length to prove that there was communism in the early gens organization? Obviously so that when opponents say that communism is contrary to human nature, he can triumphantly answer that this cannot be if once all men were communistic. It is aimed at the oft-repeated declaration that there always has been and always will be private property. Like the sectarian, the Communist dreams of a future perfection; and like the sectarian, he bolsters his dream with the picture of a perfect age in the past.

When we see this reason for the emphasis upon a golden age, we are not at all surprised to find that a main theme of the sectarians is that the coming kingdom of God is to restore the age of innocency, to bring in again the age of Adam and/ or the age of the New Testament.

To the sectarians, it is clear that the early age was essentially democratic with a free equality for all. As John Ball, the early English revolutionary and forerunner of the sects, put it:

> But when Adam delved, and Eve span,
> Who then was the Gentleman?

The differentiation of mankind into rulers and ruled, into classes, was a result of the Fall and not of the original creation of man. Winstanley speaks for all the sectarians when he declares, "But not one word was spoken in the beginning, that one branch of mankind should rule over another." Here too one sees a parallel to the Communist theory which pictures the gens organization as being not only without classes but also without a state and thus without rulers and ruled.

The sectarians also pointed out the communistic nature of the early pre-Fall period. "The earth was made to be a common Treasury of livelihood for all, without respect of

persons, and was not made to be bought and sold." [2] Here
the relation to Communism is obvious.

Along with the idea of primitive righteousness there must
go the concept of a fall. The interpretation of the Fall is a
very vital point; for upon it will depend the analysis of the
problem of how man is to be cured of the results of the Fall.
The Communists blame private property for the Fall. With
the change in the economic system, there entered into the life
of man the institution of private property, which rapidly
corrupted all the ideal conditions of primitive communism.

The closest that the sectarians come to Communism on
this point is in some aspects of Winstanley's thinking. In many
passages he speaks as if private property were the occasion
and cause of the Fall, in fact is the Fall. The following could
be from a Marxist book: "I demand, whether all wars, blood-
shed, and misery came not upon the Creation, when one man
indeavoured to be lord over another, and to claime propriety
in the earth one above another?" [3]

There is in Winstanley's thought, however, another side,
in which the Fall is occasioned by the pride of man. In the
light of this, private property is a result of the Fall and not its
cause or basis. For Winstanley, the Fall is not simply a
matter of something at the beginning of history. It is an
individual occurrence. He might be a modern theologian as
he outlines the way in which the story of Eden is re-enacted
in the heart of every man. Thus, because man falls, as Adam
fell, into the sin of pride and self-assertion, he turns to private
property, which brings further curse.[4]

[2] George Sabine, ed., *The Works of Gerard Winstanley* (Ithaca: Cornell
University Press, 1941), p. 289. Used by permission of the publishers.
    [3] *Ibid.*, p. 290.
    [4] *Ibid.*, p. 158.

Among the other sectarians the Fall is viewed in more orthodox light. It is the result of the sin of man. Some, but not all, point to the state, private property, wars, sufferings, and so forth as direct results of the fallen condition of man. How then, we may ask, does the sectarian view of the Fall differ from the more orthodox interpretations?

Actually the concept of the Fall can be conservative or radical, depending upon the context in which it is held. Down through the ages of Christianity, the dominant view was that man remained under the curse of the Fall, even after his conversion to Christianity. Original sin cursed all men and was escaped only by death. In *The City of God*, Augustine argues that God did not intend that men should have dominion over anything but the animals. But man fell, and with the Fall came the occasion of slavery and the state. As a consequence man must accept the burden of authority and rule over his fellow men. Thus, while the state with its rule of some over others cannot be said to be ideal, it is necessary in the fallen condition of men. In other words, man cannot hope to wipe out the evils that result from the fallen condition, he must adjust himself to them.

But when the doctrine of the Fall is seen in the context of sectarianism, it becomes breathlessly radical. For the sects believe that man may be redeemed to perfection. That is, the effects of the Fall may be overcome. Thus it is the duty of all Christians to cast out the effects of the Fall in their own lives and in society. Everything that is old is made suspect, for all things that we have inherited are a result of the Fall and must be overturned. The saint began to overthrow the old church and ended with the old king, the old society, and the old economic system. Milton is a good example of this as he declares that change cannot be too swift provided that it is from the worse to the better. He insists that "custom is a natural tyrant in religion and in the state, a tyrant which has an ally in man's fallen nature." [5] The sectarian view of history is thus one which sees degeneration marking the story of man from the time of the Fall, but a degeneration that is to be suddenly reversed by the action of God, just as man, the sinner, is to be converted to sainthood.

Here too is an interesting parallel with Communism which sees all history since the Fall under the curse of private property and class warfare but which holds out the hope of a sudden dawning of a new day which shall repudiate all things that are now under the curse.

THE NATURE OF SIN

Another parallel between Christianity and Communism is found in the doctrine of sin and its relevance to history. Again, the parallels are most striking between Communism and the sects where we find resemblances to the Communist theories that all of society, its institutions, ideals, religion, and government are tainted with a class ideology or, in other words, with a suppressed and slightly hidden self-interest.

Generally speaking, the sectarians did not have any elaborate doctrine of sin. They were not theologians but men faced with the practical problems of their times. They saw sin as a fact, and they attacked it regardless of where it was found or what it might cost them. They believed that they had, through Christ, found the cure for it in both individual and public life.

Quite frequently the sectarians held the orthodox Augustinian view of sin as pride or self-exaltation. Even Winstanley,

[5] Quoted by Woodhouse, op. cit., p. 50.

radical as he was, held an orthodox view of sin. He can say: "The first fruit that the created being, Adam, brought forth was the spirit of self-love aspiring to be equal with God, for every being has a disposition to promote himself. . . . This is the mystery of iniquity, the aspiring of the creature to be an absolute being like God." [6]

While essentially orthodox, however, Winstanley in particular and the sects in general denied the idea that all men are born hopelessly under the curse of Adam's sin of long ago. They believed that each man had his own fall.[7] The denial of original sin in the sense of its coming from the historic Adam is not a shallow view of the problem of sin. Rather it is a determination to face the problem. In too many orthodox circles of the day, the reference to Adam, original sin, and the Devil enabled the individual to escape the fact that *he* was a sinner. Sin was a vague something associated with evil forces outside oneself. To such complacent individuals, the sectarian cried out that Adam, the Devil, Antichrist are "within you."

In discussing Winstanley's view of the Fall, we pointed out that he had a twofold theory; sometimes he blames the Fall on pride, sometimes on private property. So, in his doctrine of sin, he has in some passages an almost Marxian identification of sin and private property. He can say: "The Nations of the world will never learn to beat their swords into plowshares, and their spears into pruning hooks, and leave off warring, until this cheating device of buying and selling be cast out among the rubbish of Kingly power." [8]

[6] *Op. cit.*, p. 81.

[7] *Ibid.*, p. 176. John Saltmarsh, in his treatise *Sparkles of Glory* (London, 1647), has a section which he calls "Anti-Christ Within Us," in which a similar idea is present.

[8] *Op. cit.*, p. 511.

Generally speaking, the sectarians saw as the worst sins those which were committed against men. As we mentioned before, their attacks upon luxuries and pleasures were usually based on the feeling that, in the midst of want, no man had the right to luxury and waste. They could be and often were petty and legalistic, but at their best they did see that violation of love was the essence of sin.

For our study it is interesting to note the sectarian recognition of the class nature of much sin. They believed that the state, the Church, and other institutions were tainted with the sin of class interest. At this point they resemble Augustine, who also saw the state as being built upon self or class interest. He charged that it was ruled by the powerful groups in a fashion not too different from that of a robber band. Nonetheless, as we have seen, Augustine felt that the state was a necessity under the fallen conditions of man and that the Christian ought to give it his support.

The sectarian attack upon the state as an instrument of sin and class, however, goes further than that of Augustine. Like the Communists, the sectarians were suspicious of the state in itself. In particular, we think of the attitude toward the state which was taken by the pacifist sects. Here there was no attempt to overthrow the state nor even to challenge it, but simply a disdain of it. The saint could not soil himself with service to it nor allow it to encroach upon his conscience. The Mennonites were even more thorough than the Quakers in their repudiation of the state. They saw that force supported all activities of the state. Thus the Mennonite could not support, by his participation, any form of civil government. Mennonites could not hold offices in any government which used force for any means. They were willing to admit that the state was ordained of God, but ordained for controlling sinners. For the saints, the state was not necessary, and they must not make use of its facilities or recognize any duties to it except the duty of complete indifference. H. C. Vedder remarks that the Mennonites were forerunners of modern anarchy rather than modern Communism.[9] In saying this, he overlooks the anarchistic element in Marx. Marx too distrusts and repudiates the state; it is an agent of oppression, unnecessary in the ideal society. Marx's difference from the anarchists is one of timing. First, says Marx, the state must be used during the dictatorship of the proletariat, and then, as the need for it disappears, the state will wither away. In other words, like the Mennonites, Marx sees the necessity of the state for the "sinners" until the "Kingdom" comes.

The sects, however, did not have suspicion and antagonism for the state simply because it is an instrument of force. They also bring charges of class interest and of injustice against it. A recurring theme of the sects is the manner in which the state is ruled by the rich and the nobility for their own interests. The laws of the state are, they claim, written by the rich for the rich. George Fox the Younger sounds almost as if he is quoting from Marx when he says:

And the poor man is thus oppressed, . . . he must be subject to the Laws which they make who are his oppressors, or else he is accounted a Rebel; so what right think you is the Oppressed like to have, when his Oppressors chuse the men who are to be the Judges of his Cause; and thus the rich men oppress the poor, and draw them before their Judgment Seats. . . . These things being considered, ye may see the unequalness and partiality that hath been chusing of Parliaments according to England's Custom, and how unlike it is that a Parliament so chosen should make England

[9] *Socialism and the Ethics of Jesus* (New York: The Macmillan Co., 1912), p. 15.

a free Nation, seeing the great Oppressors of the land, (viz.) Priests and Lawyers, and the great wicked, covetous, persecuting men are so much concerned in the chusing them.[10]

Closely joined with this feeling that the laws are for the advantage of the rich and the rulers is the realization that justice cannot be obtained by the poor since the trip through the law courts is too expensive. As John Rogers says, "The price of Justice and Law, and of recovering a man's own, is too high for a poor man, he cannot pay for it, and is thereby forced to lose it." [11]

The sin of the church also was under continual attack from the sectarians. Many of these attacks upon the church were purely religious. It had been unfaithful to Christ and had compromised his teachings. It had allowed the unsaved into its ranks and even into its highest offices. It had become an agent in persecuting the saints and destroying the freedom of religion. In short, the church had committed the unforgivable sin of becoming absorbed by the "world."

The sectarians were not simply using a rhetorical word when they spoke of the "world"; they had in mind the fact that the ruling and powerful classes had confiscated the churches for their own purposes, just as Marx was later to charge that the churches reflected the interests of the capitalists. "Ecclesiastical power," said Winstanley, "is not ordained of God but is got by crafty men from kings, to kill the truth and persecute the Saints." [12] To a considerable extent this feeling explains the deep resentment the sects felt when forced to pay taxes for the state church. Of course, it is annoying to

[10] Op. cit., p. 88.
[11] Op. cit., p. 55.
[12] Op. cit., p. 89.

have to support a church in which one does not believe, but the sectarian would have opposed the practice even if his own church had reaped the benefits; for he was certain that the Church could never be prophetic and free so long as its support came from the government. "The Sheep of Christ shall never fare well so long as the wolf or red Dragon payes the Shepherd their wages." [13] It is apparent that the charge that the churches were corrupted by the "world" was a charge against the class taint and special interest of the churches in a manner quite similar to Communist charges.

With this in mind, we are not surprised to find among the sects the Communist charge that religion is an opiate of the people. Christians long before Marx recognized that religion could be and often was used to dull the demands of the people for their just economic and social rights. As we might expect, it was Winstanley who had the most biting words to say on the subject.

The Ministers . . . lay claime to Heaven after they are dead, and yet they require their Heaven in this World too, and grumble mightily against the People that will not give them a large temporal maintenance. And yet they tell the poor People, that they must be content with their Poverty, and they shall have their Heaven hereafter. But why may we not have our Heaven here (that is, a comfortable livelihood in the Earth)? And Heaven hereafter too, as well as you, God is no respector of Persons.[14]

It is clear that the charge of "pie in the sky" is not something which is unique to the twentieth century or to anti-Christian critics.

[13] *Ibid.*, p. 387.
[14] *Ibid.*, pp. 409-10.

This general discussion of the idea of sin in the sects reveals that they, like the Communists, saw the class taint which enters into the state, the Church, and the administration of justice. The sectarian was not one to fight a hazy concept of sin nor to worry about the smaller legalistic aspects of life, although some sectarians did fall into that trap. Normally he cried out against wickedness in the highest of places and had a real understanding of the political and social corruption of his time.

Providence and Ultimate Victory

One of the beliefs of Communism which arises out of the doctrine of dialectical materialism is that the forces of the universe are moving toward the Communist goal and that whoever co-operates with these forces is working in a cause that must triumph. Furthermore, there is the insistence that mere ideals can never change society unless economic conditions are ripe for a change. In other words, powers outside man must be working with man if he is to succeed in his desires.

There is much in this that immediately reminds us of the Christian doctrine of providence. The God of the Christian system has been replaced by the impersonal force of dialectical materialism, but it is nonetheless a force which is working for the salvation of man and society. Again, however, we are primarily interested in the similarities with the sectarians.

The first striking similarity of thought between the sectarian and the Communist at this point is the certainty of victory. This was the promise which the sects proclaimed to all who would hear them. The Communist believes that nothing can stop the triumph of Communism and is not daunted by any strength which the capitalist forces may show, for he believes that time and the forces of the universe are on his side. Likewise, the sectarian was never daunted by difficulties or seemingly preponderant forces against him, assured as he was that time and the power of God were with him.

Even persecutions of the elect were for the sects signs of the time, because such persecutions heralded the near approach of the end—they were the last torments in the day of darkness. "Alas, alas, poor Precious Seed of God, ye must be tryed, abused, and most shamefully treated once more. But Wo, Wo, Wo, from the Lord God of Heaven and Earth to them that do it." [15] Likewise Marx foretold that in its last days monopolistic capitalism would make a stand in which there would be ruthless exploitation and suppression of the proletariat. "Along with the constantly diminishing number of the magnates of capital . . . grows the mass of misery, oppression, slavery, degradation, exploitation." [16] But these too are the signs of the end; for in the same paragraph Marx goes on to promise that the time is short when these sufferings begin. "But with this grows the revolt of the working class. . . . The knell of capitalist private property sounds. The expropriators are expropriated." [17] Because of this faith, both Communists and sectarians are uplifted in hope during persecution, for such treatment heralds the coming deliverance.

The sects believed that the very actions of the wicked helped the cause of the Lord, although they did not will it so. "Mysteriously it comes in and men know not how; whilst

[15] Edward Billings, *An Alarm to All Flesh* (London, 1660), p. 9.
[16] *Capital*, tr. S. Moore and E. Aveling, ed. F. Engels (New York: International Publishers, 1939), pp. 788-89.
[17] *Ibid.*, p. 789.

men act and intend their own designs in comes Christ with
his Kingdom. . . . They intended to fulfill their own wills
and the will of the people in taking away tyranny and Tyrants;
but God intended thereby a fulfilling of his will so long foretold of his little horne." [18] Here again we cannot help seeing
the striking similarity to Communism, which sees its forecast of history being worked out by men who have no desire
to do such a thing. The capitalists follow their own profit
and try to build their own wills into history, but their actions
continually, much against their wills, are leading to the
destruction of capitalism. Thus the *Communist Manifesto*
declares, "What the bourgeoisie therefore produces, above
all, are its own grave-diggers. Its fall and the victory of the
proletariat are equally inevitable." [19]

The sectarian view of history culminates, as we have seen,
with the apocalyptic hope that Christ is coming again to
judge and redeem the world. At first sight there seems to be
little in common between this hope and the Communist
belief that the proletariat must take matters into its own
hands and forcibly overthrow capitalism. Yet a closer ex-
amination reveals that there is an amazing similarity. This
was probably first pointed out by Baron von Hügel.[20] In Communism we find a secularized version of the sectarian's apocalypse.

The first note of any apocalypse is one of promise. It is
directed primarily to the lowly classes, to the exploited and
persecuted, and it comes to them with a promise of release
and salvation. Deliverance is the perennial theme of the

[18] John Rogers, *op. cit.*, p. 129.
[19] Authorized English Translation, edited and annotated by Friedrich Engels
(New York: International Publishers, 1939), p. 21. See also Engels, *Anti-
Dühring* (New York: International Publishers, 1939), p. 341.
[20] *Essays and Addresses*, Second Series, p. 273.

apocalypse, and in times of apocalyptic enthusiasm there is certainty that the day of justice is about to dawn, that already the signs of the time are pointing to the imminent approach of the end. Belfort Bax, a Marxian in outlook, shows a keen appreciation of the meaning of apocalypse for the poor. Discussing the Peasants' War in Germany, he says: "All the then oppressed classes of society, . . . all with whom times were bad, found consolation for their wants and troubles, and at the same time an incentive to action, in the notion of a Divine Justice which should restore all things, and the advent of which was approaching." [21] There was no suffering or tribulation which would not be healed in the apocalyptic future, no injustice that would be left unrighted, for the Lord was to act. In short, these people looked for a state of affairs not too unlike that which Marx promises will come when Communism is victorious.

But the apocalyptic hope is much more than just a promise of future bliss, for as such it would be little different from a belief in progress. Apocalypse recognizes that there is no easy path to the Kingdom. The way is beset with trials and troubles, and all history is the story of conflict and struggle. God is pitted against Satan, Antichrist against Christ. "There is a perpetual Antithesis and opposition that is put between the Kingdome of the world and the Kingdome of Christ." [22] The Christian is caught in this perpetual struggle, battling with Christ, suffering with him, oft defeated, oft cast down, but ever rising by the grace of God and looking with hope to the day of deliverance.

[21] The Peasants War in Germany, pp. 22-23.
[22] John Owen, A Sermon Preached to Parliament, October, 1652 (Oxford, 1652), p. 18.

Like the Communist analysis, this Christian one is dialectic, and it is a dialectic which rules out all ideas of a smooth and continuous evolutionary progress. The new age has a relation to the old but not a relation of development. It is rather a relation of contrast, negation, and contradiction.

This aspect of continual conflict reminds us of the dialectic of Marx, but an even closer resemblance to Marx is detected when we see how often the sects interpreted this conflict in terms of a class struggle. To a considerable extent, the sectarians looked upon the poor as the chosen class who had a particular destiny as the upholders of God's will and his Kingdom. Inasmuch as the sectarians were drawn predominantly from the poorer classes of society, it is not surprising that they believed that the poor had a particular mission, under God, to bring in the Kingdom and were to hold a special place in the Kingdom when it had come.

Joachim of Floris, as a forerunner of the sectarian views of history, put a great emphasis upon poverty and the special privileges of the poor. The Anabaptists carried on this theme, adding to it, however, in the revolutionary wing, a note which proclaimed that the poor were to work toward building the Kingdom by pulling down the rich. Among the English sects it was taken for granted that the rich were a lost group and that the purposes of God would have to come through the poor.

Even education was disparaged by the sects, because at that time education was a privilege of the rich. The clergy had become a monopoly of those who could afford to be trained. The refusal to believe that the call to preach followed economic lines led the sectarians to protest against education in general. That is, to a large extent the sectarian protest against education was a protest against a church which was dominated by the rich. And this protest was made by men who believed that the poor, not the rich, were the best soil for the Word of God.

Faith in the poor was increased as the sects became convinced that the poor had been used in the past for particular purposes of God. They never tired of pointing out that the chief characters of the Bible were poor men. A group of Quakers, including George Fox, writing to King Charles and Parliament, summed it up:

> And concerning what Sort of People the Lord made use of, and spake to in the Old Testament; and concerning also what sort his Son Christ Jesus made use of . . . such as were Herdsmen, Plow-men, Keepers of Cattel, Gatherers of Fruit, Threshers of Corn, Keepers of Sheep: And these were hated of the World . . . and these had not been at Universities . . . but Jesus Christ was their Teacher . . . and if he make use of the same, and such like now, be not offended.[23]

Because of this, the sectarians felt that in a time of religious reformation, like the one in which they lived, it would be the poor again upon whom God would call.

As Winstanley saw it, it was the duty of the poor to act as witnesses of the age to come. "Let the rich work alone by themselves, and let the poor work together by themselves; the rich in their enclosures, saying *This is mine*; the poor upon their Commons saying *This is ours*." [24] And to the rich he declares, "The poor people whom thou oppresses, shall be the Saviours of the land; for the blessing is rising up in them." [25]

This concept of the poor as a messianic class with the duty

[23] *For the King and Both Houses of Parliament* (London, 1660), pp. 8-9.
[24] *Op. cit.*, p. 196.
[25] *Ibid.*, p. 264.

of bringing in the Kingdom bears such a striking resemblance to the Communist theory of the duty of the proletariat to bring in Communism that one hardly needs to expand upon it. The sectarian, however, did not believe that the poor, as poor, are the heralds of the Kingdom; it is the "enlightened" poor who have been saved, who shall bring in the Kingdom. Here we are reminded of Marx's belief that it is not the proletariat qua proletariat which shall bring in Communism, but the proletariat organized and led by the "enlightened" Communist Party. What the sect is to the poor in general, the Communist Party is to the proletariat in general. It is the redemptive remnant that shall lead the whole of society to salvation.

On the other hand, there is the sectarian protest against wealth. Riches were viewed as among the chief evils of man. Partly this was an ascetic belief that only the poor are worthy of God, with a real resemblance to medieval monasticism, but it was strongly tinged with a feeling that wealth cannot be obtained except at the expense of one's fellow men. Winstanley asserts that "all rich men live at ease, feeding and clothing themselves by the labors of other men, not by their own." [26] The writer of *Tyranipocrit* puts it even more plainly: "To be rich and pious . . . is impossible." [27]

Violent language is not unusual among these writers when they are referring to the rich and ruling groups. In referring to these groups Hanserd Knollys can cry, "Blessed is he that dasheth the brats of Babylon against the stones." [28] Such language reveals that class hate and a sense of class

[26] *Ibid.*, p. 511.
[27] Quoted by W. Schenk, *op. cit.*, p. 150.
[28] A. S. P. Woodhouse, *op. cit.*, p. 233.

struggle run through the apocalyptic interpretation of history.

A further aspect of this class struggle is the belief that when the Kingdom comes, the classes will be reversed—the poor will be elevated over the rich, the weak over the powerful. Again and again the sectarians recall Jesus' words— "Many that are first shall be last; and the last shall be first."

Sometimes it seems that greater satisfaction is taken in the sufferings that are to come upon the powerful than in the rewards to the poor. But it would be unfair to suggest that such a vengeful attitude was characteristic of the sects in general. Yet even the Quaker James Naylor can say, "Oh ye great men, and rich men of the earth, weep and howl for your misery is coming." [29] Such passages are more abundant among non-Quaker sects. Obviously the fighting Anabaptists and Fifth Monarchy men are full of such declarations, as is natural in persons who are in open conflict with the powerful classes. But when we find the same forecast of doom in pacifist Quakers, we can see that the class-conflict theme runs through all the sectarians, and the promise of judgment upon the powerful and rich is an integral part of the apocalyptic world view.

A further characteristic of apocalypse is the realization that the present condition of the world is essentially evil. This is not to say that the sectarian saw no value in the world as it was, for he did. But it was not to be compared with the glories of the coming age. Just as Marx felt that there was some good in capitalism as a necessary step to Communism, so the sectarian saw much that was good in the existing order. He even granted a value to the government, but it was only of

[29] James Naylor, *The Power and the Glory of the Lord Shining Out of the North* (London, 1656), p. 9.

value for the interval before the Kingdom. Again, we think of the Communist promise that the evils of the capitalist system will not appear in the new order, which shall overcome both the good and the evil of the dying system.

The recognition of the evil of the present helps to divide sharply the apocalyptic from the modern progressive views of history. For apocalypse there is no steady advance in history that would make today better than yesterday. On the contrary, there is a deterioration and worsening of the situation; the conflict between Christ and Antichrist forces is sharpened as the end approaches. The Antichrist troops gird themselves for the fray, and the great battle of Armageddon is the climax before the final victory. This is why it will go hard with the saints in the last days. In fact, things will get so dark that the intervention of God is the only hope of deliverance that is left. "Ye have heard that Anti-Christ should come, even now there are many anti-Christs whereby we know that it is the last time." [30] "Great warres, desolations, alterations shall precede it [the Kingdom]." [31]

The comparison here with Communism is obvious. Marx too saw not a steady advance toward communism, but a growing series of economic crises, increasingly bitter battles between capital and labor, a more intense battle for survival among the capitalists themselves, the proletariat sinking in misery until finally the catastrophic revolution breaks forth and communism comes "apocalyptically" out of the crisis.

An interesting side light on the question of apocalypse is its relation to force. Logically it would seem that an apocalyptic world view would lead to a pacifist attitude, and it did in such groups as the Mennonites and Quakers. If God was to

[30] John Saltmarsh, *Sparkles of Glory*, p. 113.
[31] John Owen, op. ict., p. 19.

intervene, then there was no need for man to try to overthrow the forces of wickedness in high places. But this pacifism
did not mean inaction; it meant the feverish preparation of
oneself for the last days and the coming Kingdom; it meant
a progressive withdrawal from the world, which was doomed,
and the attempt to build a society, within society, in which
the Kingdom was foreshadowed.

But apocalypse can very easily be turned into a revolutionary
dogma of a fanatical nature. And it was so turned by Thomas
Münzer and the Fifth Monarchists. The line of logic that
lies behind this is that since the coming is delayed, it must be
the duty of the saints to take up arms and hasten it. Under
such circumstances the revolutionary is completely fanatical,
certain of the righteousness of himself and his cause, so that
he battles without giving quarter. It is, of course, to this type
of apocalypse that Communism belongs. The fanaticism of
the Communist, in revolution and in preparation for it, is to
be understood in terms of his apocalyptic view of the struggle
in which he is engaged.

There is a division among the sectarians in interpreting the
apocalypse. With some of them, the apocalypse is purely
chiliastic—that is, God is going to come personally and
literally in fulfillment of the biblical prophecies. God himself
will strike the blows for his saints. Strangely enough, this
literalistic view is held most frequently by the revolutionary
sects. They feel that their revolution will hasten or even force
the hand of God. But another viewpoint is found among men
like Winstanley, the Quakers, and Saltmarsh. Here the coming of the Kingdom, while no less a divine intervention,
comes by God's filling the hearts of individuals who work, inspired by his Spirit, to bring in the Kingdom. A good example
of this viewpoint is in Thomas Collier's words: "Some appre-

hend that Christ shall come and reign personally, subduing his enemies and exhalting his people, and this is the new heaven and earth. But this is not my apprehension; but that Christ will come in the Spirit and have a glorious Kingdom in the spirits of his people, and they shall, by the power of Christ in them, reign over the world." [32] This does not mean that these men had a progressive interpretation of history, although it can easily slip over into that kind of view and has done so frequently. They see the conflict in the world, the worsening of events, the suddenness with which the Kingdom comes, as we have pointed out. They feel that they are on the verge of the breaking in of the Kingdom and are aware of the judgment that it involves. It is also plain that this form of apocalypticism will not lead to inaction but to action. When the Diggers began to dig and plant the commons, they were acting in the light of this kind of apocalypse. It was an apocalyptic act, demanded by the moral requirement of the coming Kingdom and performed by men who felt that their actions were needed both to herald it and to help bring it in.

We are now in a position to look back and sum up this section. Marx differed from the nineteenth-century thought with his catastrophic view of history, the idea that times grow worse and reach a crisis before they become better. These ideas were all strange to the thought of Hegel and to the theories of progress which were the ruling interpretations of history in the time of Marx. The nineteenth century found the meaning of life in the hope that the world was steadily improving and that it was moving inevitably into an era of earthly perfection. Time, it was believed, would inevitably solve the age-old problems of man. Scientific reason, spread

[32] A. S. P. Woodhouse, *op. cit.*, p. 390.

by public education, was progressively replacing strife and conflict. Marx agreed with this view of progress inasmuch as he too looked for a perfect society in the future. But his picture of the catastrophic in history had no place in the optimism of the times. Basically, therefore, Marx is closer to the sectarian thought than he is to the secular thought of his own age. It is not necessary to claim that Marx drew directly upon the insights of the sects, but certainly a parallel form of thinking can be detected.

Communism and the sects agree in seeing a world which is, at present, highly undesirable. Not only are there injustice and exploitation, but there is a tendency for these forces to grow. History is the scene of a catastrophic conflict between the opposing forces of "good" and "evil," and as the conflict of these forces intensifies, the hope is grasped that the solution of the struggle is imminent. This conflict is one not of persuasion but of annihilation. There can be no compromise of a lasting nature between Christ and Antichrist, between capitalist and proletariat. One must be destroyed.

Despite the injustices and conflicts of history, there is a force working in and through the acts of history which is, regardless of what men do or fail to do, leading man to a final solution of the conflicts of history. The duty of man is to understand this force, co-operate with it, and reveal its tendencies to others. The sects recognize this force as God; Communists call it dialectical materialism.

In this battle, by a perverse logic, war, revolution, poverty, despair, persecution, all lead to, in fact are necessary for, ultimate victory. Just when things seem most hopeless, there is really the most ground for true hope. By something of the same logic, it is the weakest, poorest, most persecuted classes which will triumph, while the richest and most powerful will be cast down from their places of prestige.

This comparison brings out the essentially religious nature of Communism. Of course the sectarians and Communists worship different deities and look to different forms of assistance in their victory, but both groups look beyond themselves to a power with which they can co-operate in certain victory. It might be objected that the Communist is, or tries to be, scientific in his approach, while the sectarian was superstitious or driven by an unquestioning faith. Such an objection would not be made by one who had read the sectarians. They did not know the modern meaning of "scientific," but they tried to use their intelligence, their reason, and their systematic study to analyze the meanings of the Bible and of the events of their time. They tried, in short, to be scientific. Like Communism, the sects used the best methods at their disposal to understand the course of history and the part they could and ought to play in it. Both produced a committed faith to things still "hoped for" and "unseen." Psychologically speaking, there is little difference between faith in God and the prophecies of the Bible and faith in dialectical materialism and the prophecies of Marx. If, therefore, we define religion in terms of the psychology of the believer rather than in terms of what he believes, it is certain that Communism is religious. Likewise, if we define religion as belief in a power greater than man, which assures man that there will be a victory of good over evil, the Communist is religious.

Despite all these similarities, there is a difference between Communism and the sectarians. And it is a difference of such a decisive nature that Communism appears as a caricature of the sects and not an inheritor of the tradition. We shall have more to say on the point, but in passing we mention it here. The power working for the solution of history is, in Communism, a purely historical force, and the salvation of history is within history itself. Whereas the sectarian looks for history to be saved, the Communist expects history to save itself. The "God" of Communism is not a God of righteousness and justice so much as it is a God of inevitability. We shall see later how these differences help to explain why the sects contributed to democracy while Communism tends toward totalitarianism.

THE KINGDOM OF GOD UPON EARTH

Joseph Needham points out that in the history of Christian thought, there have been four distinct theories about the time and place of the kingdom of God.[33] It has been thought to exist "here and now," as we have seen the medieval world thought with regard to the Church. It has been proclaimed that the Kingdom will exist "here but not now." This, as we shall see, is the view held by the sects. In direct opposition to this sectarian view has been that which declared that the Kingdom exists "now but not here." Many sectarians, particularly Quakers and Mennonites, came to this verdict. This can be a very conservative doctrine, for all practical purposes identifying the Kingdom with an afterlife. It exists up in heaven, and we shall go to it, but it will not come to us here. Or this may mean that we can enter the Kingdom now in mystical contemplation. Society does not enter into the Kingdom, which is known only by the individual. Lastly, the Kingdom has been held to be "not here and not now." In

[33] See John Lewis, et. al., eds., *Christianity and the Social Revolution* (New York: Charles Scribner's Sons, 1936), p. 424.

this sense, it is viewed as the coming reign of God, not on earth but in heaven after the Last Judgment. Obviously all possible combinations have been held. Most of these versions, with the exception of the second, would be branded by the Communists as "pie in the sky."

There can be little question but that the great majority of the sectarians looked forward to the Kingdom, and they looked for its appearance on earth. This is immediately obvious in the case of the revolutionary groups. The Anabaptists believed that they had set up the Kingdom in Munster, and Venner's Fifth Monarchy revolt was to set it up in England. But the other sectarians likewise looked for it on earth.

The early Quakers came closest to having an interpretation of the Kingdom as "now but not here." Inasmuch as this became almost completely orthodox among later Quakers, it might be thought that this was the ruling view among the early Quakers. But such would not seem to be the case, for one finds many passages in which they insist that the Kingdom is coming upon earth. It would seem probable that even among those who spoke of the Kingdom as being here and now within the believer, there was also a belief that it was still to come in power among all men. George Fox, while speaking often of the Kingdom as now dwelling among the saints, has passages which point to a coming Kingdom upon earth. Writing to the Pope, he can say:

Now is the Lord coming to take Vengeance upon you, and with that he will rule you and smite you under, and bring you lofty ones from your seats and abase your pride, and take the glory to himself, and deface your glory and honour. . . . Your wickedness hath grown to the full, your time draws to an end, that the Lord God will be avenged on you. . . . The Lord God of heaven and earth is come to reign and rule whose kingdom is without end, in whose hand all kings are as the waters, and thou, and thy images and relics.[34]

Whatever else this passage may mean, it would seem to indicate that, for Fox, the Kingdom was something more than God dwelling in the hearts of believers; it was also to be manifest in the world, where it would soon overthrow the powers of evil.

There is no doubt, however, that an earthly kingdom was a part of the gospel of the other sects. In fact, Winstanley goes so far as to charge that one of the chief lies which the preachers had passed off on the people was the lie that the Kingdom was not to come upon earth. "O ye hear-say Preachers, deceive not the people any longer by telling them that this glory [of the Kingdom] shal not be known and seen, til the body is laid in the dust, I tel you, this great mystery is begun to appear, and it must be seen by the material eyes of the flesh." [35] In short, as Winstanley saw it, one of the chief features which distinguished the sectarians from the average churchmen of his day was the belief that the Kingdom was to come on earth.

When the Kingdom came, it was, of course, to solve all of the problems of man, right the ancient wrongs, and restore man to the position he had held before the Fall. Among other things, this meant that there would be a classless equality of men in the new age. When the Anabaptists believed that they had set up the Kingdom in Munster, they sent out their letter proclaiming, "The poorest of the poor who are here

[34] *The Works of George Fox*, IV (Philadelphia, reprinted 1831), 247.
[35] *Op. cit.*, p. 170.

among us, and who were formerly despised as beggars, now
go dressed like the noblest of the land." [36] Despite the fact
that their leader, Jan of Leyden, set himself up as King of
Munster, he still showed a new concept of kingship when
he took over the despised and loathsome task of executioner.
This act symbolized the belief that a king was one who
served. It took the sting out of the remaining class differences.

This equality bordered on ideas of communism and became
an explicit communism in men like Winstanley. He pictured
the coming Kingdom in communistic terms, as is evident
from the following quotation:

When this universall law of equity arises up in every man and
woman, then none shall lay claim to any creature, and say, *This is
mine, and that is yours.* . . . There shall be no buying or selling
. . . but the whole earth shall be a common treasury. . . . There
shall be none lord over others, but everyone shall be a Lord of
him self.[37]

Not all of the sectarians, however, went the whole length of
communism, but those who did not at least saw the new age
bringing an end to poverty and unjust inequalities.

Experiments in communal living have had a long history
in the Christian Church. The earliest Christians for a time
shared their property equally with one another. Because
of the sects' desire to be like the primitive Church this naturally made a deep impression upon them. Even after this early
practice was abandoned, there remained in the Church men
like Chrysostom and Ambrose who attacked established ideas
of private property and demanded a sharing of wealth. The
medieval monastery was a miniature communist community.

[36] Quoted by Johannes Janssen, *History of the German Peoples at the Close
of the Middle Ages,* V (St. Louis, 1903), 459.
[37] *Op. cit.,* p. 184.

The medieval Church managed to produce a number of communistic sects. Helen White has shown that the English Church, in the sixteenth century, had a radical "social gospel." [38]

One of the chief declarations of the sects which bordered on communism was the insistence of the essentially sinful and unchristian situation which existed while some were rich, living in luxury, and some were dragged down in a burdensome poverty. The coming Kingdom would abolish this kind of inequality, they believed. George Fox, the gentle Quaker, can become as bitter as Marx himself when he deals with such a situation.

> Your blind men, widows and fatherless children, [are] crying up and down, lieing in every corner of your streets; crying up and down half a dozen together . . . crying for bread, poor and lame, is not this a shame to your Christianity? . . . Men and women are so decked with gold and silver in their delicate state. . . . Surely you know not that you are all of one mould and blood, that dwell upon the face of the earth. Would not a little out of your abundance and superfluity maintain these poor children. . . . He that despiseth the poor despiseth his Maker.[39]

Fox is here on the border line of communism, although he does not draw the conclusion that all men ought to be completely equal nor that there should be a common ownership of goods. He is not as close to Marx as he is to the later slogan of England's Labor Party—"Let none have cake until all have bread."

There are important differences, however, between this

[38] *Social Criticism in Popular Religious Literature of the Sixteenth Century* (New York: The Macmillan Co., 1944).
[39] *The Works of George Fox*, IV, 135.

sectarian hope for some form of communism in the coming kingdom of God and the Marxian-Communist hope for a communistic future. The sectarian ideal of communism is based entirely upon the Christian doctrine of brotherhood. Because men are the sons of one Father, it is an insult to God if some men are starved while others dwell in luxury. Marx repudiates an ethical or theological appeal, in theory at least. Marx wanted communism because it was "scientific."

Furthermore, the sectarians had a fear of wealth as such. They knew the grave temptations that went with wealth, and they did not ask luxuries for themselves or the poor. The kingdom of God was not a future time of luxury. The sects wanted only the necessities of life for all. Communism, of course, sees no meaning whatsoever in a fear of wealth; it desires an ever-growing amount of wealth for everyone in society.

It is clear that there is a strong resemblance between the kingdom of God looked for by the sectarians and the kingdom of communism promised by Marx. There are considerable differences in detail, but in principle the two hopes are the same. Both desire and expect a coming age, on earth, in which there will be no more class divisions, no more poverty and exploitation, in which the poor shall find their rightful place, and in which the age-old strifes and troubles of men shall be surpassed in a new age of bliss and perfection. Both hope for the coming age in which all wars will cease, not only the wars between nations but also the conflicts and bickerings that divide men from their brethren.

There is another similarity between the Kingdom of the sects and that of Communism. This is, however, a similarity with only a minority of the sects. Among some of the sects there was the idea of a dictatorship in the Kingdom. The Anabaptist revolutionaries and the Fifth Monarchists wanted a kingdom ruled by the saints. These concepts remind us of Marx's dictatorship of the proletariat. As Marx saw the proletariat ruling only until it should have wiped out the last elements of capitalism, likewise the dictatorially minded sects only expected to have to rule the short time before all who were not saints should be destroyed or converted. In other words, both groups looked for an interim in which society would be ruled for its own good by those worthy of ruling.

Against any such ideas stood men like the early Quakers, Winstanley, and the Levellers, who wanted no minority rule. It made no difference who the minority was. Winstanley said of the Kingdom, "The greatest offence will be this; for any to endeavour to raise up some few to rule over others and to set up particular interest again." [40] He clearly meant this to apply to any attempt to set up a rule of the saints as well as to any other form of rule. For one man to rule another was unjust and had no place in the Kingdom for Winstanley and the other sectarians like him.

The Communists and all the sectarians were agreed, however, that the ultimate aim was a society in which all men would be righteous (for the sectarian because sin would be overcome, for the Communist because private property would be abolished) and in which no government would be required. Men would live in peace and harmony with one another without need of an overruling force to prevent their aggressive attacks upon their fellows.

This chapter has enabled us to see that there are several

[40] *Op. cit.*, p. 192.

areas in which Communistic and Christian views of history
find a meeting point. Yet even in the points of contact there
are both subtle and obvious differences. We are now prepared to turn to the task of criticizing the Communist interpretation of history from the Christian perspective. In doing
this, we shall find that, despite the sympathy the Communists
have shown for the sects, sectarian Christianity is of aid to us
in refuting the claims of Communism.

WHAT IS THE STRENGTH OF COMMUNISM?

WHEN he is faced with a struggle, the wise man will carefully weigh the strength of his enemy. Jesus once said to his disciples, "What king, going to make war . . . , sitteth not down first, and consulteth whether he be able with ten thousand to meet him that cometh against him with twenty thousand?" In the modern struggle with Communism it is imperative that Christians weigh the strength of Communism as a religious alternative to Christianity. Otherwise we may go into battle unprepared.

Many persons qualified to do so have weighed the relative strength of the Communist and democratic countries in the military and economic realms. It is our purpose to compare their strength in the spiritual realm. This cannot be done unless we honestly admit those truths and values which are represented by Communism and which are the clue to its ability to win religious devotion from millions of followers around the world today.

My thesis in what follows may be put very simply. Communism, growing up within a Judaeo-Christian culture, has expressed certain values of that culture. This is demonstrated by the similarities between Christian and Communist views of history. But if Communism expresses certain truths of Christianity, it lacks others. The lack of these other truths does much to invalidate the truth that it does have. Christianity is, therefore, to be preferred as a system of thought and a way of life. The strength of Communism arises, however, in part at least, from the failure of many Christians to assert and live those Christian truths which Communism does maintain. At these points we will find that quite frequently the sectarian movement of Christianity has preserved the Christian truths which other Christians may have lost. Consequently, to answer Communism, we must draw upon the strength of both the church and sect types of thought.

All Institutions and Activities are Marred by Sin

One of the true insights of Communism is its understanding of the manner in which all human institutions and activities become perverted to the selfish use of particular groups. This is illustrated in the Communist doctrine that the state, the Church, the intellectual pursuits, and the morality of any society are used to promote the class interest of those who are powerful enough to capture them. The Christian doctrine of sin has always understood this fact also; it is, for example, made clear in Augustine's analysis of the City of the World. But it is the sectarians who have been most insistent in proclaiming this aspect of Christian faith.

The sects were not fooled by the claims to divinity or privilege which were made by any of the institutions of their day. There was no institution which was beyond their criticism, be it the monarchy, the state, or the Church. They were keenly aware that self-interest had laid its fingers over man's most sacred institutions and that the best of them had become the tools of private interest rather than servants of the public good. Thus the sectarians saw that the state was never purely and simply an impartial administrator of a divine or perfect justice but was also a weapon of selfish interest and class greed. John Rogers is quite typical as he says:

And when once they had got possession of the Law, their first work was to secure themselves and their own greatness by a guard of Laws against the Liberties and Freedom of the people, in so much that our Cannon being thus turned upon us, they charge us with thunderings threatening of us for traytors and Rebels by the letter of their Lawes, if we but stir a step towards our freedom.[1]

Christianity has always had a deep suspicion of the state. In the New Testament itself there are two contrasting views of the state. On the one hand there is the oft-quoted declaration of Paul, "Let every soul be subject unto the higher powers. For there is no power but of God . . ." (Rom. 13:1; see also verses 2-7). But in the New Testament there is another strain, best seen in Revelation, where the state is the beast and the Christian's duty is to resist it at any cost (Chapters 17-18). Jesus himself was critical of the state—"They who are accounted to rule over the Gentiles lord it over them; and their great ones exercise authority over them. But it is not so among you" (Mark 10:42, A.S.V.). These two ideas have been held in an uneasy equilibrium throughout the history of Christianity. Augustine, in his *City of God*, recognizes certain positive values of the Empire, but ultimately it is the City of this World, opposed to the City of God. There can be an area of co-operation between the two cities, but obviously if there is any conflict, it must be the City of God which is obeyed. The history of the Middle Ages is the history of the continual efforts of the Church to establish its independence from and even a dominance over the state. The close of the Middle Ages saw the rise of the national states of Europe and the consequent subduing of the Church to them. Frequently the charge is made that Protestantism gave itself over to

[1] *Op. cit.*, p. 48.

the state, but it is equally true that while Protestants were becoming the right arms of the princes, the Roman Catholic was also becoming the tool of the sovereigns in Catholic countries. The only consistent voice raised against the alliance of Church and state was that of the sectarians.

The twofold idea of the state in the New Testament is often seen as a confusion of thought or a contradiction. Sometimes it is suggested that in the days of Paul the Church was protected rather than persecuted by Rome, so Paul taught submission to ruling powers; while in the time of Revelation the Church was being persecuted, and so it attacked the state. This neat solution of the double view of the state overlooks a very important point. Even in the teachings of Jesus there is implicit the later tension between the ideas of submission to and defiance of the state. "Render . . . unto Caesar the things which are Caesar's; and unto God the things that are God's." (Matt. 22:21.) These words of Jesus are not, as often interpreted, a simple solution of the claims of the state and Church. They at once recognize and challenge the state. They insist that the things which belong to God cannot be rendered unto Caesar. Further, the life of Jesus was the scene of tension between himself and the state. He referred to the King as "that fox" (Luke 13:32), and finally it was Rome which put Jesus to death. Yet he refused to sanction rebellion. Thus in Jesus himself there is one strain which gives the state its due and refuses to revolt against it, and yet another strain which defies the state. This is not due to a basic contradiction in the teachings of the New Testament, but rather it is the result of a basic tension in the nature of all states. For "government is at once the source of order and the root of injustice." [2]

[2] Reinhold Niebuhr, *Faith and History* (New York: Charles Scribner's Sons, 1949), p. 220.

The state is necessary to social life under the conditions of sinful humanity. It is the barrier against anarchy. But it is always more than just the preserver of order; it is also the protector of special interests against the universal good.

The sectarian and Communist critique of the state is of continual validity wherever any state makes absolute claims to power. Orthodox Christianity has, generally speaking, concentrated upon the sayings of Paul about obedience to the state and has emphasized the value of the state in keeping order. It has failed to see that the same force which protects order also can, and often does, protect injustice. Historically, Catholic and Protestant orthodoxy (some Calvinists excepted) have put greater emphasis upon obedience to state authority than they have put on the duty of defying the state. In fact, rebellion has always been held under considerable condemnation, regardless of the injustice involved. In practice, this view has often identified the Church with the entrenched social groups and placed it against the forces of progress. There is still a widespread tendency in Christianity to sanction the state and its actions with little question. This is most tragically clear during the twentieth century in the refusal of any church to defy its government in time of war. At this point the Christian pacifist has inherited the sectarian ideal of refusing to bow before the claims of the state. The Church continually needs to listen to the protest against the state which is understood by the sects and Communism.

Interestingly enough, the place where today the Communist and sectarian understanding is most needed is in the very state which first claimed to have become Communist. No state is making any more totalitarian claims to rule the whole life of its citizens than is modern Russia. Marx proclaimed that so long as there was a state, it would be the agent of class oppression and not the guardian of public good. He is being proved correct by Russia. There has never been a state which has more openly protected the rights of a particular class and at the same time made such grandiose claims to be interested only in the public good. The class protected in Russia is, of course, a new one, not foreseen by Marx; it is the class of state bureaucrats, the Party members.

Recently a news item came out of East Germany. A Lutheran pastor had been arrested by the Communist government because he had declared that the Christian must obey God rather than the government. This incident, so typical of our times, is significant. It reveals the provisional nature of Communism's wisdom at this point. The Communist believes that all states but the Communist ones are under a higher judgment. This in turn illustrates the basic conflict between Christianity and Communism. Christianity is loyal first to God and only secondarily to any human institution. Because God cannot be enclosed within any institution, all institutions are under judgment. Communism, recognizing no transcendent providence over history, but rather a providence immanent within history, believes that this providence is identified with the Communist-inspired proletariat. As a result, there can be no judgment over its institutions or achievements.

The Church, of course, has not always lived up to its basic principle of primary loyalty to God alone. In fact, there have been many times in history when the Church claimed for itself an absolutism that can be claimed properly by God alone. For example, the followers of Augustine who, forgetting his qualifications, identified the kingdom of God with the Roman Catholic Church came close to this kind of absolutism. Despite this fact, there is still a basic difference between Christians' making their organization absolute and the Communists' making their achievements absolute. In the Communist philosophy there is nothing to prove the Communist wrong; he must desert his philosophy to find anything higher than his state or party. The Christian who falls into such false absolutism has, in his own basic faith, the antidote to it. We know from history that every absolutizing of the Church has been challenged from within Christianity itself.

The sectarian and the Communist (so fars as it goes) sus-spicion of the state is valid. It must ever be a part of the Christian message. But the sectarian appeal is not completely valid by itself. It too loses the tension found in the New Testament. Both Marx and some of the sectarians fall into the utopian illusion that in some future time the state will be unnecessary. This is part of the failure of these groups to understand the radically sinful condition of man. They fail to see that the exploitation which makes use of the state would be completely free and unchecked without a state. The state is a necessity for the control of the predatory instincts of man, but it is not a sacred institution as such and can become the protector of the very forces that it is supposed to check. This is the reason for the tension of the biblical view toward the state and the reason that both orthodox Christianity and sectarianism can become wrong if they lose either side of the tension.

Understanding the manner in which particular interest captures the places of power, Marx and the sectarians alike had no hope that the possessors of these positions would suddenly change their ways and use their powers to advance society or that they would calmly allow mankind to progress without a struggle. The sectarians set themselves to battle with the powers-that-be with as much resolution as the Communist has set out to overthrow capitalism. Some sectarians actually took the sword; others, like the Quakers, did not take the sword, but they set themselves sternly to oppose the rulers. The later liberal idea of a smooth, progressive application of the ideals of love to society is often hinted at in the earliest Quaker writers, but it is essentially strange to them and is denied by the apocalyptic judgment which they preached. The Kingdom remained for them the act of God and not a gradual attainment of man.

Whereas progressive liberalism has hoped for progress through the general education and enlightenment of man, the sectarians and the Communists understand that it will take more than persuasion and education to unseat the powerful from their places of domination. In this sense we must understand the sectarian note of apocalyptic judgment upon the rich and powerful.

Again the validity of this analysis is demonstrated by the country which claims to be led by Marxian principles. The great fact about post-Revolutionary Russia is that the powerful groups have shown no tendency whatsoever to allow the state to wither away. Quite the contrary, they have been steadily increasing and maintaining its autocratic power. Trotsky, speaking of the Communism of Soviet Russia, says:

Of Party democracy there remained only recollections in the memory of the older generation. And together with it had disappeared the democracy of the Soviets, the trade unions, the cooperatives, the cultural and athletic organizations. Above each of them reigns an unlimited hierarchy of Party secretaries.[3]

Then Trotsky goes on to ask a pertinent question:

[3] *The Revolution Betrayed*, tr. Max Eastman (Garden City: Doubleday, Doran & Co., 1937), pp. 99-100. Used by permission of Pioneer Publishers.

Why, from 1917 to 1921, when the old ruling classes were still fighting with weapons in their hands, when they were actively supported by the imperialists of the whole world, . . . why was it possible to dispute openly and fearlessly in the party about the most critical questions of policy? Why now, after the cessation of intervention, after the shattering of the exploiting classes, after the indubitable successes of industrialization . . . is it impossible to permit the slightest word of criticism of the unremovable leaders? [4]

The question might have been an easy one for Trotsky to answer, drilled as he was in the theories of Marx. Was it not Marx who had declared that no ruling class would ever give up its powers without a battle, that no education or enlightenment would cause a group to relinquish voluntarily the power that exalted it above others? Why, therefore, should Marx or Trotsky have expected the rulers in the dictatorship of the proletariat to give up their positions of power and let the state wither away? And why should Trotsky be surprised that, when the commissars had replaced the tsars, they should act like tsars? The answer is, of course, that Marxians have fallen prey to their own ideology, which, without foundation, believes that a change in the social system will remove the inherent evil of man. They have failed to see the stubborn manner in which sin is a part of man's nature regardless of the social system.

The sectarians, or at least most of them, were much more realistic at this point. Some of them, like the Communists, wanted a dictatorship, not of the proletariat but of the saints. Its result would have been identical with that of Soviet Russia. But the wiser of them understood that since man used positions of power to exploit the common good, the only solution

[4] *Ibid.*, p. 108.

was to make these positions of power subject to the control of all men in a democratic manner. The greater realism of the sectarian over the Communist is apparent in the following passage from John Rogers:

We must find out the Rise of good Lawes, which appears plainly to be from the people, who being most sensible of their own burthens are most capable of making Lawes for their own ease and welfare. . . . The genuine interest of Lawes in their originall is to curbe and keep in (principally) the princes, not the people; the rich, not the poor; oppressors, and Tyrants, not others of the people, to bridle great ones who are most Lawless, and to keep Governours within their due precincts.[5]

Here it is clear that Rogers recognizes that any group which is not subject to the people as a whole is bound to use its power for its own purposes and against the good of society. The Communists recognize this truth as it applies to capitalism but fail to see that it also includes the Communists themselves. Here we have one of the reasons why the sects, for all their similarities to Communism, led to democracy while Communism has led to totalitarianism.

The Communist and the sectarian, seeing that all man's social structures are corrupted by self-interest, understood that each stage of man's progress is also a decline. In short, the efforts of man to climb the ladder of progress are never unambiguously successful. The Marxians saw this clearly, and it was implicit in all the doctrines of sin held by the sects. Yet modern believers in progress have completely ignored this fact.

The truth of this concept is tragically clear, however, to anyone who realistically faces modern history. For example, take man's development of science. Here surely there is, if

[5] *Op. cit.,* pp. 45-46.

there is anywhere, an unalloyed step forward. What but good is there in man's learning to control nature for man's welfare? Yet the control of nature found by science is a control of nature not by all men, but by a few, and the consequence is that the possibilities of concentrated power also grow with science. What begins as the control of nature by man ends all too often as the control of some men by others. Consequently, it is precisely the modern age of science which has made possible the modern form of totalitarianism. The radio, press, and movie have been used to mold and subdue the minds of men as Nebuchadnezzar or Peter the Great never could have done. The possibilities of a successful revolt against the Soviet government are far fewer than were the possibilities against the tsars, because the Politburo has weapons of force and power which cannot be met by peasants with pitchforks or even by workmen with rifles. A revolutionary underground can hardly hide the weapons necessary for a modern revolution until the time is ripe for revolt.

Even in democracies, the growth of science has made a greater and greater centralization of power necessary. Some form of socialism is without doubt necessary to give all men a voice in the centers of modern power. Yet democratic socialism cannot give a real voice to all men; it must still divide men into the bureaucrats and the workers, and never the twain shall meet. Our age is faced as no other has been with the problem of power, for the simple reason that there is so much more power to use today than ever before.

So it is that this age, which has prided itself on gaining control over nature, has almost completely lost its control over history. As C. S. Lewis has suggested, "Man's conquest of Nature turns out, in the moment of its consummation, to be

Nature's conquest of Man. Every victory we seemed to win has led us, step by step, to this conclusion. All Nature's apparent reverses have been but tactical withdrawals." [6]

The Communists and sectarians who recognize this truth have a sobering word to speak to the optimism that swept the intellectuals of the late nineteenth century.

Here, too, some sects were more realistic than the Marxians, for they saw, as the Marxians do not, that this decline applies to all historical advances. Only God can bring the kingdom of complete justice, free from taint. But the Marxians apply it to all advances but one; there are to be no drawbacks to the last great advance of Communism itself.

CRITICISM OF RULING-CLASS ETHICS

The dominant group in every society develops a type of ethical behavior which is considered to be the norm for the whole society. This ethic may be called the ethic of respectability. No person can be respectable if he rises above or falls below this standard. The respectable ethic is always pictured as the ideal and perfect ethic and is usually given a religious foundation. At many times in history the Christian Church has found itself apologizing for and defending the respectable ethic of the hour, as if it were the true Christian ethic.

The ethics of respectability change from time to time, but they retain certain characteristic features. For one thing, they frown most severely upon any deviation from the crowd. The ideal individual is never the one who is different, never the man who stands alone for principles, never the voice crying in the wilderness. Again, the respectable ethic always protects the *status quo*. The worst sins are those which shake the pres-

[6] *The Abolition of Man* (New York: The Macmillan Co., 1950), p. 43.

ent order of things. Thus the respectable person is always law-abiding and has no patience with the man too weak to live up to the law or the high-souled individual who sees the possibilities of a higher and better law. The respectable ethic has its origin in the upper classes, the ruling groups; and from them it spreads downward, being imitated by all classes which are striving to find a position of respectability. Only the outcasts dare to flout its ideals, and they do so at their own peril.

Jesus fought an almost continuous battle with the respectable morality of his day as he found it represented by the Pharisees. The Church that bore his name, however, was not so true to its mission of criticizing later forms of pharisaical respectability. In due time the Church itself became respectable, a bulwark of law and order. It forgot that Jesus was a deviationist from the popular way, that he attacked the pretensions of respectability, declaring that the harlots and sinners would precede the respectable Pharisees into the Kingdom. It also forgot the radical love ethic which Jesus put into the place of respectability.

Sectarianism restored the prophetic Christian protest against respectability. The Quakers attacked the ruling-class ethic of their time at its very heart. They refused to take off their hats in the presence of their "betters," or to use the respectful "you" instead of the familiar "thee." Most shocking of all, they would not take oaths or serve the state in time of war. Even the Quaker refusal to wear the clothes in fashion set them apart from the respectable majority. The modern age sometimes fails to see the meaning of these actions, thinking of them as legalistic literalism or plain eccentricity. They were nothing of the kind. They were the means used by a pacifist group to defy the whole ethical and social system which was accepted as absolute. It was their way of dramatizing their belief that the ethic of the day was not Christian. The other sectarians may not have used the same types of behavior, but their beliefs were identical with that of the Quakers. They repudiated the ethic that was preached in the churches and repudiated it in the name of a thoroughgoing application of the Sermon on the Mount to all aspects of life. The established ethic of respectability was, they felt, weighed in favor of the rich; it was not based upon universal norms of righteousness, but upon particularized expressions of selfish interest.

Karl Marx took up this same sectarian protest against respectability, which he termed "bourgeois ethics." There are times when Marx comes close to being nihilistic in his repudiation of all ethical norms; but at other times he tries to put a new ethic in the place of the old, an ethic which is "scientific" and hence nobler than the old one, an ethic which does not discriminate against large groups of the population. In practice, the ethic of Marx has often meant nothing more than a way of justifying any means which may be used for hastening the proletarian victory. The fact remains, however, that there is a validity in the criticism which Marx makes of bourgeois ethics, even as there is in the sectarian protest against the ethics of the church. Whenever Christians forget the radical nature of their ethic and compromise with dull respectability, they need to be awakened by someone, even if that someone is a Karl Marx who stands outside the Christian tradition.

Social Justice

Throughout the Bible the great theme that unites the prophets to the apostles is the theme of social justice. Before God, all men are equal, and they must be treated as such.

When the powerful exploit the weak, or the rich the poor, it is sin before God and the gravest possible sin. "Relieve the oppressed," cries Isaiah. "Judge the fatherless, plead for the widow" (Isa. 1:17), while Amos warns, "Ye kine of Bashan, that are in the mountain of Samaria, which oppress the poor, which crush the needy, . . . the Lord God hath sworn by his holiness, that, lo, the days shall come upon you, that he will take you away with hooks, and your posterity with fishhooks" (Amos 4:1-2). Similar quotations abound throughout the whole Old Testament, and the theme reappears in the New Testament. There can be no question but that the Christian religion is a religion that preaches social justice and deplores any kind of special interest at expense of the poor.

The Church, however, often has neglected this aspect of the Bible. Allying itself with the respectable ethics of the time, backing the *status quo* against any rebellion, it has failed to be impressed with the sufferings of the poor. When official Christianity has been blind to the demands of the poor for redress, and to the attacks of the rich upon the rights of others, it has been necessary for the sectarians to raise their voice in reproof and to cry out for a more just society. In our day we have seen Marxian Communism rise up to sound the same note.

However much we repudiate Communism, we cannot ignore that here Marx spoke with a voice that Christianity itself ought to be sounding forth. We cannot remain silent and let Communism alone speak of justice and equality, brotherhood and mutual respect in social affairs. It is one of the tragedies of our time that we have become so frightened of being called "Communist" that we often are afraid to speak forth for justice. I hope to prove before I am finished that Christianity and Communism are essentially in opposition to each other, but the Church must be very wary of allowing itself to be identified with those opponents of Communism whose real purpose is not to fight the totalitarian aspects of Communism but who wish to defend the *status quo* against the legitimate criticism of its injustices which Marx makes.

No Christian has a right to condemn Communism until his own passion for social justice equals its passion and supersedes it. To paraphrase the saying of Jesus, "Except your righteousness shall exceed the righteousness of the Communists and the capitalists, ye shall in no wise enter into the kingdom of God."

Again, however, we come across the interesting fact that the so-called Communist country—modern Russia—must be severely criticized by the ideals of social justice. For social injustice is still a ruling feature of the Soviet economy. André Gide was an enthusiastic follower of Communism and a great exponent of Russia's experiment until he made a trip to Russia and found there the very injustices and inequalities which he had repudiated in capitalism and which had driven him to Communism in the first place. He says, "What distressed me most [in Russia] was not what was not yet perfect, but rather to find there everything from which I had always fled at home—the privileges which I had hoped abolished forever." [7]

It is significant to find the Russian system criticized by a confirmed Marxist upon the basis of the Marxian appeal for social justice. This could be Marx writing about the England of his day, but it is Trotsky writing about the Union of the Soviet Socialist Republics:

According to the conditions of its daily life, Soviet society is already divided into a secure and privileged minority, and a

[7] See Richard Crossman, ed., *The God That Failed* (New York: Harper & Bros., 1950), p. 180.

majority getting along in want. At its extremes, moreover, this inequality assumes the character of flagrant contrast. . . . The members of collective farms . . . live as formerly in the old huts with their calves and cockroaches. On the other hand, the Soviet dignitaries complain in the press that not all the houses newly constructed for them possess "rooms for house-workers"—that is, for domestic servants. . . . 15%, or say 20% of the population enjoys not much less of the wealth than is enjoyed by the remaining 80 or 85%.[8]

In 1940 a decree was passed in Russia which raised the tuition for secondary schools and universities, with the result that some 600,000 students of the poorer classes had to leave school. A recent Reuter's news report summarizes what a group of Swedish newspapermen found in Moscow. The newsmen reported that there was more snobbery in Moscow than in noncommunist Sweden. What impressed them most was the difference between the elegance of clothes worn by the wives of officials and the down-at-heel type of dress worn by the typists and factory girls.

Facts like these are precisely the kind that should be used widely by Christians in their attack upon Communism. It would take from Communism the initiative which it has gained by picturing itself to the exploited peoples as the great defender of social justice, and it would put the Soviets on the defensive. One hears little of such criticism, however, perhaps because such attacks demand as their honest consequence a criticism of our own inequalities and social injustices. It is more pleasant to criticize Russia at the points where we are strong, rather than where we too have our weaknesses.

[8] *Op. cit.*, pp. 116, 142. Used by permission of Pioneer Publishers.

The Poor As Agents of Justice and Deliverance

The Christian faith has always understood, as did the Jewish prophets before it, that the poor had a special messianic task to perform in the world. This understanding was united with the realization that the rich were, by their very position, made incapable of being truly righteous. Ministers of upper-class churches have worried long in their attempt to explain away Jesus' teachings about the camel and the needle's eye (Matt. 19:24), while they have ignored the implications of Dives and Lazarus (Luke 16:19-31). The same apologists have always preferred Matthew's version of the Beatitudes to Luke's, preferring "Blessed are the poor in spirit" (Matt. 5:3) to "Blessed be ye poor" (Luke 6:20). The fact is that the Bible recognizes what Aristotle and others have missed—that the creative forces in society must come from the bottom of the social order, because the upper classes are blinded by the interests which they are defending and cannot see the greater good for fear of losing what they have.

Arnold Toynbee sees this principle clearly established in history. "It were uncommon for the creative responses to two or more successive challenges in the history of a civilization to be achieved by one and the same minority." [9] In fact, Toynbee finds here one of the causes of the breakdown of civilizations. The creative minority which has overcome one major crisis and risen to power, ceases to be creative, tries to protect the *status quo*, and is made incapable of meeting a new crisis. Henceforth it will use its power and position to put down the new forces which might have the answer to the new crisis. In this new crisis, either the old forces must be

---

[9] *A Study of History*, ed. D. C. Somervell (New York: Oxford University Press, 1947), p. 307.

destroyed by the new or else the civilization itself will fall.
There is thus historic proof of the correctness of Jesus' oft-spoken phrase to the effect that "the last shall be first and the first last."

This truth has continually been blurred and obscured by the church, which does not like to face the fact that the future lies not with the classes which now support the church but rather with the classes that are rising. The sectarians, however, caught again this principle and refused to allow the ministry to remain the monopoly of the rich. They insisted upon the equality before God of the poor with the rich. They preached again the gospel ideal of the destined duty of the poor.

Karl Marx saw this truth and made it his central theme. Salvation for now and all future times lay in the hands of the proletariat. As in the Christian sectarian tradition, there was the belief that the poor were destined for the great things, not because they were in any special sense more righteous, but simply because, being poor, their eyes were not blinded to reality like those who worshiped their wealth.

Further, there was the recognition by Marx, as by the sectarians, that the poor were going to continue to be exploited until they did something about it for themselves. History is the scene of the struggle of opposing forces. The poor are on the side of justice, not because they are more just than the rich but because their claims for their self-interest coincide with a greater justice than do the similar claims of the rich, and because their claims more often coincide with the greater good of society.

While Marx has come close to the Christian position at this point, he carries his creed too far. He makes the particular class of the poor today into the saviors of all history. He fails to see that the moment the poor become rich, they have ceased to be poor and have lost the provisional righteousness that was theirs when they were in the position of the oppressed. This has been painfully illustrated in Russia, where the rise of the proletariat to power has simply replaced one set of Russian oppressors by another. The revolutionary party has replaced the tsar. Against the tsar it had justice on its side as the poor and oppressed group. But now that it is in power, it is the oppressing group, committing injustices similar to those of the tsar.

The Christian sects were more radical than Marx at this point. They were suspicious of wealth as such. Much of their ascetic note, as we have pointed out in a former chapter, was really a method of expressing their social passion, their refusal to sanction luxuries in the midst of poverty. But the sects also recognized the grave moral dangers involved in the possession of wealth as such. This is something which seems so strange to our modern world that we can hardly admit it is anything but nonsense. And yet there is a truth here which has been illustrated so often in the pages of history that we cannot afford to ignore its implications. Neither the proponents of capitalism nor those of Communism have begun to come to terms with this danger. The capitalist theorists have refused to recognize it at all. The Communists have recognized it in their enemies but have not believed that it applied to them. Most forms of modern Christian thought completely ignore this aspect of their gospel. The sectarians seem to have been the last strong voice of warning on this subject to have been raised in our society.

CRITICISM OF THE CHURCH'S FAILURE TO BE CHRISTIAN

Down through their history the sects have acted as the conscience of the Church. The church type refuses to be exclusive; it opens its doors to all men, regardless of their spiritual stature. If they wish to be in the Church, they are accepted. Frequently they are in the Church only in the sense that they have not been put out. They have been baptized in the Church but have seen little of it since. The church type feels that by staying in society, refusing to withdraw itself exclusively, it can best hope to have a real and decisive effect upon the whole of society. At the risk of becoming simply another aspect of culture, it tries to keep in contact with the world. The result is that inevitably the church type tends to become watered down to the level of society as a whole, so that to be a "Christian" loses all meaning. The Church can no longer speak a word of prophetic judgment upon society, for it is society itself. At such a moment the witness of the sect is indispensable.

The sect is exclusive, demanding that a man be a practicing Christian before he join the group, insisting that the Christian must be different from the world and withdraw from the ways of society at large. The sect can and does stand in judgment over society, because it is different from society. But more important still, it reminds the Church of the real nature of the gospel and forces the Church to return to something of the original purity of its message. The service of the sect to the Church is continually needed if the Church is not to lose its Christianity completely in the ocean of secular culture in which it must sail.

The gospel of Christianity is a message of "good news." It is a way of life which can overcome evil, which calls man to wipe out injustice, and which hopes for a better time to come "on earth as in heaven." But the church, in its tendency to fit into society, is always losing this radical note and thus comes to terms with the status quo, refusing to disturb it with any radical criticism. The church begins to sit complacently in the presence of injustice and often is actually allied with the very forces of oppression.

The sect recalls the ethics of the Sermon on the Mount and challenges the church with having forsaken this ideal. The sect charges that the church's doctrine of sin is such as to make men satisfied with their present condition of morality and hence complacent. For it teaches that all men are sinful and that not even the saved can become perfect. This theory allows men to sit languidly amidst their sins while failing to strive for greater perfection of life and character. The church not only causes man to be satisfied with the *status quo* of his individual life, charges the sect, but it also makes man satisfied with the social *status quo*. In short, says the sect, not only is the church not Christian, but it is an actual hindrance to man's becoming truly Christian; it is an opiate.

The great charge that Marx brings against religion, of course, is that it is an opiate. That is, it provides a transcendent escape which causes the mass of people to ignore the real reasons for their miseries and to refrain from doing the things that might improve their lot. It promises "pie in the sky" to all who accept the present injustice without complaint or rebellion.

There can be no question that insofar as the Church is guilty of this—and it often has been guilty—it is untrue to its central ideal. It needs to hear the voice of conscience, even if that voice belongs to Marx. No Christian can deny the truth of the charge which Marx makes, but he can insist that where it is true, it is a perversion which has always been attacked from within Christianity itself. At this point Christians can become too apologetic. There is no room for complacency, but nonetheless Christianity has made important contributions to the material welfare of man and to the greater justice between man and man, all of which Marx refuses to recognize and even the sects minimize.

In all of this we need to face the fact that Communist triumphs are made possible, in part, by the failures of Christians. For such failures we must repent. The want, injustice, and oppression which Communism uses as steppingstones to power are the results of the failure of Christians to be Christian. Where Christians have fought such evils and cast them out, Communism can make no appeal. Repentance is sorely needed in the midst of a struggle with Communism in which self-righteousness grows on all sides.

Nevertheless, it must be pointed out that in their criticism of the church, the sects and Marx forget one thing. They both owe a great debt to the church. Were it not that the church nourished the Christian gospel through the centuries, there would be no basis from which the sect could arise. No sect has ever been able to build a permanent and enduring organization without becoming more and more of church itself. In fact, it seems to be the fate of the sect to become a church or else to die out. Similarly, Marx owed much more to religion than he ever admitted. We have seen many similarities between Christian and Communist thought. Marx could never have arisen except in the background of a Christian culture. His moral appeals presuppose an age steeped in Christian tradition.

A Dynamic and Prophetic Interpretation of History

The sectarians caught the note of prophecy in their view of history and thus restored a vital element of the Christian faith that was all but lost in the Church from Augustine to Joachim. We have seen that the biblical faith was centered around a conception of a dynamic history which was moving toward a goal, with a purpose and a culmination. There was, however, a continual tendency in Christian thought to substitute the nonprophetic Greek or oriental view for the Christian. Christianity became more and more interpreted in terms of the salvation of the individual soul from the historical process, rather than in terms of the biblical view, which included salvation of the historical process.

This idea of the salvation of the soul apart from the historical process is what so often caused Christianity to deserve the charge that it was an opiate of the people. If the salvation of the soul for heaven after death is made the primary purpose of religion, and if the soul can be saved regardless of the historical situation in which it finds itself, and particularly if it is taught that earthly privation and suffering are good for the soul, then obviously religion becomes an opiate. Thomas Münzer seems to have been the first sectarian to challenge this concept by declaring that conditions within history could be of such a nature as to hinder the salvation of the soul. Later Winstanley made the charge that such religion was a means of fooling the people.

With the oriental soul-salvation theory of religion there naturally goes a conservative interpretation of history. The Kingdom exists now; that is, nothing new or better is expected of the future than we have in the present. Where it was believed that the Catholic Church was the kingdom of God, nothing new could be hoped for. Since the main purpose of God was the salvation of souls and since the Church was sufficient for that, why look for anything radically better in the future?

Tillich has drawn an interesting parallel between this type of thought and political conservatism in general. The political conservative always looks back to some event (usually a revolutionary one) as the final event in which the meaning of history is fully expressed. As a result, he believes that any future change cannot have any basic importance or make any really significant improvement on what is already here. Tillich uses the Daughters of the American Revolution as an illustration of the conservatives who "in the name of the revolution in the past, try to prevent forever any kind of revolution in the future." [10] An identical attitude of worshiping a past revolution while working to stop all future ones is found, of course, in the present Russian bureaucracy. Christians fall into the same error when they identify the beginning of the Church with the founding of the Kingdom.

It is over against this conservative, otherworldly view of history that the sectarian protest was first raised by Joachim, who declared that the third age, the age of perfection, was still to come. History was not dead nor stagnating; it was moving toward a future culmination. The biblical view was again sounded forth.

Communist and sectarian views resemble the biblical in their assertion that the world, as now seen, is at variance with the world as it ought to be and as it was intended to be. In other words, there has been a fall. At present, history is the scene of violent and vicious struggle between forces of good and evil. But history is not a meaningless flux to be escaped; it is of utmost importance, heading for a destined fulfillment. History is not meaningless nor doomed to unending separation from its essential nature. There is a providential guidance over history which will bear it to its fulfillment.

The biblical view has further parallels with the sectarian

[10] *The Protestant Era* (Chicago: University of Chicago Press, 1948), p. 24.

and Communist in that it sees judgment coming upon the powerful groups of society and a special mission for the lowly and downtrodden. Lastly it agrees in seeing the meaning of history presented in certain acts and events of history. For the Bible and the sects, this meaning is made clear in the revelation of God through his dealings with the Jewish people and finally in the life, death, and resurrection of Jesus. For the Communist this meaning is made clear by the rise of the proletariat, the class destined to end all classes. The modern Communist sees the Russian revolution as a still further point of revelation of the meaning and destiny of history.

Probably the greatest strength of Communism lies in the fact that it has caught something of the eternally valid prophetic view of history. We live in an age which borders on despair but hungers and thirsts after hope. It is its prophetic message of hope that wins devoted followers to Communism. There is much lacking, however, in the Communist view which is essential to the prophetic and to the Christian views. In the next chapter we shall discuss these inadequacies.

Conclusions

This chapter may be distasteful to the fanatical opponent of Communism inasmuch as it has found validity in certain concepts of Communism. He will be only slightly mollified by the fact that many of these insights have been used to criticize modern Communist Russia. Of course, the Communist will be infuriated at the suggestion that Communism may not be complete or have any deficiencies in comparison with Christianity and will consider very perverse any attempt to find values in Communism because it agrees with Christian belief at certain points.

Nonetheless, it is by no means traitorous to find good in

Communism. Reinhold Niebuhr has said that Communism is much more dangerous than was Nazism because it is better.[11] To some this might seem another of the eternal paradoxes which Niebuhr is supposed, by his critics, to love. Actually it is a very clear fact. Given two forces which are essentially evil, the most dangerous will be that one which has enough residual goodness to win consecrated support and which can satisfy some of the basic needs of humanity. Because Communism can do both of these better than did Nazism, it is a far more dangerous enemy. If we are going to defeat Communism, we have to understand its truth as well as its falsehood, or else we will underestimate it. Those persons who refuse to see anything but complete evil and darkness in modern Communism are doing no service to the anti-Communist cause, for they fail to understand the complex nature of the battle.

It follows from seeing the value of Communism that a program of pure negation is doomed to fail in its attempt to overcome Communism. We have to do more than be against it. There must be a positive side to our attack, an attempt to achieve the values which Communism promises.

Basically the battle with Communism is a battle for the souls of men, a battle for enthusiastic dedication to ideals. The reason that Communism is making such a strong appeal to millions today is that it does have a half-truth, and people are turning to it when they do not find even a half-truth in the alternatives presented to them. To people suffering under want and oppression, people for whom life has lost its meaning, Communism offers a message of hope and redemption. If no one else offers them a program which

[11] Niebuhr has used this in lectures to his students at Union Theological Seminary.

can take into account their deeper needs, we shall continue to lose millions to the Communist cause until finally all our atomic bombs and our techniques will be useless to stem the rising tide. Too many anti-Communists are becoming Maginot-line minded, putting their faith in the negative forces of military power rather than in the positive methods which would undermine Communism at its source. Such methods remind us of persons who would try to wipe out mosquitoes by swatting them rather than by spreading oil on the waters in which they breed.

IV   A CRITIQUE OF COMMUNISM

In this chapter we are going to concentrate upon those aspects in which Christianity challenges the adequacy of Communism as a way of life. Among other things, I hope that this chapter will cast light upon the reasons why, for all their similarities, Communism led to totalitarianism while the sects led to the founding of modern democracies.

THE MATERIALISTIC INTERPRETATION OF HISTORY

It is usually taken for granted, particularly by those outside the Christian faith, that the first Christian criticism of Communism will be brought against its atheism and materialistic interpretation of history. Actually, such is not the case. The term "atheist" is very difficult to define. Ironically enough, it is always the theist who must define the term and not the man who calls himself an atheist. The atheist is one who denies what the theist believes, and hence the theist must define what is denied.

Two meanings of the term atheist are evident. In the first the term means anyone who denies the prevalent theories about the nature of ultimate reality or God. In the second atheism means that form of thinking which can find no meaning in the flux of events. It believes that man's values have no support or validity except that which man chooses to give to them. Such atheism has no hope for victory of good over evil and finds nothing with which to be ultimately concerned or to which it can make an unconditional commitment. Niebuhr shows that this second meaning of atheist does not fit Communism when he says, "Its ostensible atheism is less significant than its idolatry. It worships a god who is the unqualified ally of one group in society and against all others." [1]

Similarly, there is no Christian argument against the materialistic interpretation of history insofar as it is a scientific theory. Christianity, properly understood, has no quarrel with any legitimate scientific theory. (The Christians who have tried to set Christianity against evolution and other theories of science have been pretty generally discredited.) A scientific theory must be challenged on scientific, and not religious, grounds. One of the great errors that were held by both sides in the science-religion controversy was the mistaken conception, drawn mainly from Greek philosophy, that if something is shown to have a material basis, then God is ruled out. There have been many who felt that Christianity must always be on the side of idealistic philosophies and against materialistic ones. Such is not the case. Christianity sees as many weaknesses in a philosophy of idealism as it does in one of materialism. Christianity can do no more than say Amen! to many Communist criticisms of Hegel, for example. Hegel and the idealists seemed sometimes to forget that man lives on earth in a human body. Idealism has generally ignored the Christian doctrine of the resurrection of the body and has overlooked the implication of the doctrines of Creation and Incarnation.

The doctrine of Creation, particularly when linked with the doctrine of the Fall, means that we cannot identify the actions of nature with the acts of God, for God is not the natural process; he is the Creator of it. But it certainly does

[1] Faith and History, p. 211.

not mean that when science finds a natural explanation of some event, formerly considered divine, the divine significance is taken out of the event; for God is still the Creator and thus the ultimate basis or cause of the event.

The Marxian theory of dialectical materialism does not necessarily rule God out. As Alexander Miller puts it:

It is no part of the Christian thesis that ideals have been more powerful in history than brute facts; as if God were able to manipulate ideas, but a bit helpless when it came to the sphere of the material and economic, so that to acknowledge the power of hunger and class-interest and natural and biological causes was to rob Him of His prerogatives.[2]

The Christian who is interested in re-establishing the biblical view can thus have a keen appreciation of the Communist criticism of pietistic religion and idealistic philosophies which do not understand the importance of the material facts of life and history for the spiritual development of man.

There is a value and truth in Marx's theories. He did reveal the fact that in any age the social life of man is lived within the framework of the economic means of production, even as an artist must paint within the framework imposed upon him by the nature of his paints and canvas. The validity of Marx at this point is recognized by a number of thinkers who would not agree with any of the conclusions which Marx draws from it. Further, Marx shows that much of the thinking which man believes is independent reasoning actually is based upon the economic substructure of life. This is in harmony with the Christian doctrine of original sin.

[2] The Christian Significance of Karl Marx (New York: The Macmillan Co., 1947), p. 80.

There would seem, however, to be serious scientific reasons for being careful about an unqualified use of the materialistic dialectic. It is not our purpose here to make criticism of Marx in the economic realm, but we might point out that many economists have marshaled a host of incidents and situations which defy the Marxian interpretation and have shown that there are serious economic laws which Marx has failed to take into account.[3]

An important criticism of Marx, for our purposes, lies in the manner in which predictions based upon his materialistic interpretation have failed. One of the most striking has been the way in which the proletariat has continually refused to give up national loyalties to join the "Workers of the World." Nothing was more disillusioning to the followers of Marx than the manner in which the workers of all countries refused to part with national policies during the First World War.

Another disillusionment for the Communist has been the way in which workers have clung to their religious convictions and have frequently put them before their "proletarian welfare." A dramatic illustration of this occurred when Russia was fighting for its life against Nazism. It was found necessary, despite some twenty-five years of Communist indoctrination, to use the appeal of Russian nationalism and the Orthodox religion to raise the morale of the people for the battle. The slogans of Marx, Engels, and Lenin had to make room for the slogans of homeland and religion.

Furthermore, the reaction of an individual or a society to

[3] See H. J. Laski, *Communism* (New York: Henry Holt & Co., 1927), pp. 84-88; M. M. Bober, *Karl Marx's Interpretation of History* (Cambridge: Harvard University Press, 1927), chap. XVII; and W. N. Loucks and J. W. Hoot, *Comparative Economic Systems* (New York: Harper & Bros., 1938), pp. 261-69.

the problems of economic conditions seems to depend upon something other than economic conditions. The same economic conditions will defeat one group and inspire another to new efforts. The problems which Marx clearly saw in capitalism have seen a variety of solutions or attempts at solution. Marx took it for granted that there could be only one solution and result—Communism. Actually there has been the answer of Nazism and fascism in some countries, reformed capitalism in countries like the United States, democratic socialism as in England, and a widespread co-operative movement as in Sweden. Communism has appeared only in Russia and China without foreign invasion, and in neither of these countries did the capitalistic system exist to bring about the conditions which Marx believed necessary for Communism.

Today the means of production have made this one world, but we are faced with the grave problem that the material basis of one world does not make a world fellowship any more than putting two men into the same room makes them friends. The material situation simply creates the necessity for a solution, but the solution takes more than just materialistic manipulation. There is a spiritual problem of man which, although it is not divorced from the materialistic, nevertheless must be treated in its own right and not just as an appendage to the economic forces of life.

There is a basic problem in historical study which probably keeps it from ever becoming a science in the sense that Marx thought that it was. The problem is this: History is a great mass of facts, all of which can never be included in any historical study, even if they are known. The historian must pick out the facts which he believes are significant. Now the facts of history do not, as a general rule, come labeled "significant." Obviously a revolution or an achievement like the

Magna Carta are important. But when one looks behind
these to find the social forces which brought them into being,
he must use his own judgment of what facts to study. To do
this, he must have a presupposition of what is important. He
cannot prove this presupposition by the facts; for it decides
what facts he considers. Consequently, historians look at the
facts and "prove" their presupposition, which is not surprising, since the presupposition has picked the facts to study.
The Marxians have not looked at facts and then proved the
primacy of the economic; they have presupposed the primacy
of the economic, and as they look at history, they leap over
facts of religious belief and practice, morals, and so forth,
and concentrate on the economic. Naturally they "prove"
the primacy of the economic.

The Marxian interpretation can never be refuted by looking
at the "facts" of history. The Marxian will always dig up
other "facts" which he will insist are more basic. Dialectical
materialism can be challenged only by assuming a different
perspective. The Marxian perspective, I believe, is based upon
too shallow a view of human nature. It can never hope to
understand man or the nature of history.[4]

HISTORY WITH AN END BUT NO CONSUMMATION

From the Christian point of view, the Communist interpretation of history is inadequate because it presents a view
of history which has an end without a consummation. It has
an apocalypse without a transcendent power behind it. It
cannot answer the deepest questions about life or man, so
that it falls into despair or idolatrous complacency.

[4] For a brilliant discussion of the limitations of objectivity in general, see
E. T. Ramsdell, *The Christian Perspective* (New York and Nashville: Abingdon Press, 1950), chap. I.

F. J. Woodbridge has expressed the essential problem of death. "Although death is a natural and inevitable event, it persists in being strange and unintelligible. It is life's end and not its consummation. It puts a stop to man's existence without completing it." [5] This is a problem which threatens all meanings of life. But the same problem hovers over history, too.

History also faces an end which will not be a completion or fulfillment of man's story upon earth. It is certain that some day the curtain will fall on man's history. Perhaps it will fall soon in atomic destruction which man brings onto himself; perhaps it will come thousands of years hence when the evolution of the sun will make the earth unfit for life. However or whenever it comes, it will write "finis" to the story of man without culminating or consummating that story. It will not bring anything to a climax or solve any problems, or mean any final victory. It will be just the end.

This forces man to face the possibility that history is meaningless. Man is not going anywhere, except to meet a blind destruction somewhere beyond the shores of today. Yesterday, by chance, man came crawling out of the primeval slime, and for a brief day he has struggled, suffered, and fought. But tomorrow he will pass whence he came, and it will not matter that he has been nor what he has done. History is but "an unpleasant interruption of nothingness." Every historical achievement of man is covered with the shadow of impending meaninglessness.

The German physicist C. F. von Weizsäcker reveals the implications involved here when he points out that the nineteenth century saw two important scientific theories ad-

[5] *The Son of Apollo* (Boston and New York: Houghton Mifflin Co., 1929), p. 209.

vanced. They were the second law of thermodynamics and the theory of evolution. The result was that

the theory of evolution quickly became the battle cry of every modern mind. The Second Law, on the other hand, remained a technical detail of physics; subterfuge was used to evade its application to the world as a whole. For the prospect of the heat death of the world, however far off in the future, would have shaken the faith that life has meaning.[6]

Thus the modern world used evolution as the cornerstone for a myth of progress and ignored the physical laws that denied that myth.

All living philosophies of man have to come to terms with this basic problem. Some philosophies have solved it by denying a meaning to history and have found the meaning of life in terms of the otherworldly salvation of the individual. This was the view of many Greek philosophers and is the view of Buddhism. It has been also the view of many types of Christian thinking, but it is not the view of the Bible. Others, and here we find Communism, try to solve the problem by believing that before "finis" is written to the story of man, this story will be fulfilled by history within history.

The real power and appeal of Communism lie in its promise of an essential meaning to the history of man. It promises that fulfillment shall come before "finis." Deliverance is coming from the evils of history; history is going some place, and the place to which it is going gives meaning to the journey by which it arrives there. The coming age is at once the goal and the fulfillment of the historical process. It gives meaning to living in the present and hope for the future.

[6] *The History of Nature* (Chicago: University of Chicago Press, 1949), p. 70.

The holders of such a view must look for the fulfillment of history in the future, and the near future at that. They must feel that they are living in the penultimate stage of history, with the new day already casting its first beams over the horizon. Man does not demand that he set foot in the promised land; he is content to see it from afar, but he does wish to feel that at least his sons will enter it. He does not wish it to be so far in the future that it will not be reached by those in whom he is vitally interested.

It is one of the chief weaknesses of Communism that it subordinates the present to the future. The present life is recognized to be a nightmare; the future life, however, will be all that any man can ask—heaven upon earth. Generations of men have been born, lived, died, and been buried without their feet ever coming close to the promised shore. But their sufferings will be redeemed when the human race achieves the goal. As individuals they will not be there to take part in the culmination of history and the fulfillment of its meaning, but they will have helped to pave the way for it, and this alone is their consolation, even if they do not know for what they have suffered. But when stripped of its idealistic-sounding phrases, this simply means that the men of this age are but the tools of the future. Men no longer have a value in and of themselves but only as they contribute or fail to contribute to the future age of perfection.

Arthur Koestler tells how in a Communist writers' conference, after several hours of speeches about the brave new world of the future, André Malraux asked, "And what about the man who is run over by a tram car?" The question brought a painful silence, after which someone lamely remarked that in a perfect socialist transport system there would be no such accidents.[7] In other words, there was no answer in the Communist philosophy to the question, and there cannot be. The man who dies fighting for the faith can have the grim consolation of knowing that he died for the cause; but the man who dies a pointless or accidental death, what of him? Yet he is the symbol of the millions who have lived and died before the coming consummation. Their lives are all without meaning or significance.

With a theory like this, it is no wonder that the Russian Communists saw nothing inconsistent in starving several million peasants in 1932 in order to sell wheat to buy machinery. After all, since millions had suffered and died in the past for the completion of history, why become suddenly anxious about a few million more on the very dawn of Utopia? Communism cannot escape the logic that when you subordinate the present to the future and make the former a means to the latter, you are subordinating the individuals of the present to the individuals of the future. The concept of the eternal value of man is lost. This is a reason for the Communists' low estimate of the individual, which we shall discuss in greater detail in the next section.

The Communist view runs continually on the verge of despair. The cause of this despair may be twofold. A Communist may begin to doubt the accuracy of Marx's predictions, since already he has been proved wrong in many things. Perhaps he was wrong in forecasting a future of Communism. Perhaps the future lies with fascism. Perhaps a monopoly capitalism, armed with weapons Marx could not foresee, will be able to crush the proletariat. Or, more evident still in an age like ours, perhaps men will be destroyed by atomic war-

[7] *Op. cit.*, pp. 122 ff.

fare before Communism can really blossom in Russia or be established elsewhere. This is one avenue of despair ever before the Communist unless he is completely intoxicated with the slogans of Marx.

A second type of despair, more frequent, is found when the Communist awakens to the unpleasant fact that Communist Russia is hardly the land of anyone's dreams. One day he sees Russia as a terrorized police state which uses power politics, is guilty of international imperialism and war mongering, and which still has all the inequalities of capitalism remaining. He sees it as a land in which labor has less power in determining its hours of work and wages than it has under capitalism and in which anti-Semitism is used when it seems convenient for official policies. He decides that if this is the culmination of history, then man is indeed a wretched creature, and he is traveling nowhere except to his own destruction. This is a form of despair that has caught many a Communist in these last few years, the despair of realizing that the Marxian heaven, the goal of history, is a place of unlivable horror. Where now is he to find the meaning of history?

When the Communist is caught upon either of these two prongs of despair, he is in a serious spiritual vacuum. History and life have lost all meaning. Today we see a multitude of these disillusioned Communists. Some of them have become bitter reactionaries, either in public affairs or in disgruntled seclusion. Others have made unscrupulous attacks upon their former comrades for purposes of self-aggrandizement. Those who have managed to struggle up to some steady faith are few.[8]

---

[8] An interesting study of a former Communist who is searching for a philosophy to replace the faith which he once had in Communism is found in Arthur Koestler. See especially his The Yogi and the Commissar. See also

Despair is not, however, the only—and perhaps not the usual—reaction to the dilemma outlined here. Even more typical is the refusal to face the fact that Russia is not the utopian heaven that fulfills the meaning of history. This results in a blatant, self-righteous exalting of the Soviet Union at any cost and in face of all facts. It means the refusal to face the weaknesses and shortcomings of the land which is supposed to have Communism.

When the goal of history arrives, obviously its claims are totalitarian; nothing can be higher than it or sit in judgment over it. In Marxian theory Russia represents just this kind of fulfillment; it is "beyond the revolution." This explains why so many Communists and fellow travelers outside Russia, despite their evident high idealism, have been such docile dupes of the ruthless Russian imperialism of the last few years. They could not question the good faith or rightness of any Russian action without acknowledging that the bottom had dropped out of the faith that gave meaning to their lives. They could no more stand against Russia than the average Catholic could break with the pope or than the fundamentalist could criticize the Bible. It would mean giving up their religious faith.

It is difficult for the modern world to see fully the flaws in Communism at this point. As Reinhold Niebuhr has demonstrated in his book *Faith and History*, all modern philosophies, however much they differ from one another, have essentially the same interpretation of history. This includes many popular interpretations of Christianity as well as secular types of thought. All these views share the belief that the pas-

---

his novels. Crossmann, *The God That Failed*, presents case histories of several such disillusioned followers of Communism. See Whittaker Chambers' dramatic book, *Witness*.

sage of time must bring salvation from the ills that now plague man. They find the meaning of life in the faith that the culmination of history, the perfect society, will come within history to bless man before his time on earth comes to an end. Differences among the modern philosophies are primarily differences as to how the fulfillment of history is to be attained.

These differences are extremely important, of course. For example, Christianity can work with the humanist, who believes that democracy and education are the highroads to the era in which all man's problems will be solved. The Christian will believe that his humanist friend is naïvely mistaken, but they will still have enough in common to make co-operation possible and profitable. But recent years have made it evident that there is no hope of profitable co-operation between Christians and Communists, even when for the moment their goals seem to coincide. Furthermore, we are not falling into that popular error of supposing that everyone who has beliefs in common with an extreme position must go all the way to that extreme. The worst features of Communism can be, and probably will be, escaped by the other modern views.

Nevertheless, despite the important differences among modern schools of thought, the similarities are such that few outside the Christian tradition can see the full weakness of the Communist interpretation of history. So long as it is believed that man is heading for salvation within history and that the meaning of life lies in the inevitable building of a better earthly society, the weaknesses within the Communist system will reappear, albeit in a less drastic form.

Here the Christian faith, both in its Augustinian and sectarian forms, appears in sharp contrast to the Communist. The apocalyptic world view of the sects does not mean much to our rational world, which has been brought up and fed upon ideas of progress that have many of the weaknesses of the Communist view. But in former days life has gained meaning from the belief that Christ is coming to set up his Kingdom. Of course, the doctrine has fallen into misuse, and this is why it is neglected in Christian circles today. It can become a mere crystal-ball gazing into the future with endless arguments as to who, on the present scene, is the Antichrist and so on. We still remember the Millerites of the last century, who, believing that they knew the day and hour of the Lord's coming, gave away their possessions and gathered on the hills in their white robes to await the Lord. Their disillusionment turned most thinking Christians away from all forms of apocalyptic faith. But such interpretations are perversions of apocalypse.

Essentially apocalyptic thinking is based on the faith that God is in control of history. With this conviction, necessary to biblical faith, it becomes painfully evident that the times are out of joint; the existential situation of man is in contradiction to his essential nature; there has been a fall. Such a contradiction is intolerable; it cannot be final; it must be changed; God must act. Thus one is apt to feel that he is in the "last times" and that "the Lord is coming." Basically, however, this is not a prediction about the future so much as it is the recognition that the judgment of God is over all historical achievements. It is the faith that no matter how chaotic the times may become, the last word is not with the chaos nor with the forces of evil, but the last word is with the God revealed in Jesus Christ.

Apocalyptic views have been given a partial justification insofar as history has shown that the empires of power have fallen into destruction. But there has been no complete vindication, and these thinkers know that there can be none until the end of history—that is, until the kingdom of God appears.

The apocalyptic thinker, however, does not scorn or overlook history, for he knows that history is the field for the battle of Armageddon, that is, the scene of the struggle between good and evil. History is not to be denied or escaped; it is to be fulfilled.

The sectarian apocalypse expressed these truths which need to be held by all Christians. We may dispense with much of the sectarian imagery and the biblical literalism in picturing the end of history, but we must still cling to the basic principles of the apocalyptic view.

This view does not sacrifice the individual of the present to the future, for the dead shall be raised, and all the saints will dwell in the coming Kingdom. The apocalyptic view escapes despair because it does not need hope of earthly success. The Communist must cling to the hope of bringing in Communism in the foreseeable future, even if that future is more remote than his own life. He can hardly expect to keep on fighting for a losing cause if there is no hope that it will ever triumph. The apocalyptic thinker needs no such evidence, for he does not expect to bring in the Kingdom anyhow. It is the gift of God. Such a thinker works, counting not the cost, even when, by all historical standards, that cause for which he works seems doomed. He has faith that his efforts will not be in vain but will find their fulfillment in the final fulfillment of history. He can act as the conscientious objector who, being told that his views were very fine and idealistic and that when the kingdom of God came, they would work, drew himself up and replied, "For me the Kingdom has come." It is a paradox of life that this spirit, which does not look for worldly success, often does contribute most to the advancement of history. It is ready to lose its "life," and when it does, it may find it again. That is, it takes the risks that have to be taken if a greater good is to be achieved. The fact, however, that it is a risk causes the prudent man to pause, and in pausing he may lose even the partial good that he has.

Apocalypse is the view that expects events to get worse before they get better. It knows that history is a scene of conflict with the Antichrist arising in the "last days." There is no expectation that history will become gradually better before the consummation. Consequently, the apocalyptist is not dismayed at any reversal; no time can be so dark that it destroys his faith. It is such a man whose feet will remain most firm in the hours of hysteria and fear. He will continue to stand when others about him are losing their footing.

Lastly, apocalypse should guard against the mistake of glorifying any historical achievement, for it knows that all historical achievements are under the judgment of God. This was illustrated well by the sectarians in Cromwellian England. Like the Russian Communists after 1917, they had triumphed over the old order. They might have thrown a halo of sanctity around their revolutionary achievement as the Communists have done in Russia. But they did not. For them there could be no totalitarian claims by any historical achievement. No regime could be above judgment and criticism, for it was God who judged all things, and before God the Commonwealth was seen as less than the kingdom of God. They began to challenge the new tyrannies of Cromwell. Their ultimate allegiance was not with history; it was to God; and therefore no historical achievement could become heaven, and no historical regime could become God, as they have in Russia.

These valuable insights of the apocalyptic faith have frequently been marred with errors. I have mentioned the Millerites as an example of the error of literalism. Historically we know that the sects fell into this and other errors. The sects did not, as Communism does, expect history to fulfill itself. They escaped the despair and self-righteousness that come with such a view. But they did share with the Communists the expectation of a future perfect age upon earth. This error results from their failure to realize that the apocalyptic faith which they held meant that the Kingdom was beyond history, meaning also beyond earthly existence. When the kingdom of God comes, it ends history. As long as man remains man, his dreams of an age of perfect justice will be unfulfilled. All the Utopias that he builds will remain under the ambiguities of sin and historical existence.

Although the sects were not misled into the belief that the Cromwellian revolution had brought in the Kingdom, many of them did expect that another step from the Cromwellian state would be the Kingdom. Some did make the mistake of thinking that they had achieved the Kingdom. This explains many of the extravagant claims and acts of the Munsterites. Further, while their biblical views enabled the sects to keep a basis of judgment over their attainments, the sectarian belief that the Kingdom was coming on earth, combined with their conviction that they were the forerunners of it, gave them utopian ideas about the nature of themselves as the heralds of that Kingdom.

There are great differences among the sects at this point, as some of them fell more easily into the danger than others. The pacifist sects, refusing to fight for the Kingdom or to use force to bring it, may have had their illusions about the ability of pure love to regulate society, but at any rate they knew that no society in which coercion was used was the kingdom of

God, and hence they could see clearly through any pretensions which might be made by successful revolutionists. The Mennonites completely repudiated the city of Munster as an expression of the kingdom of God. Where the sword of the rulers was still red with blood, the Kingdom had not come; of that the Mennonites were sure.

We have seen that their sense of God guarded many of the sects from identifying their achievements with the kingdom of God. We have also seen that when the sectarian view is secularized, as in Marx, it is open to the most serious of perversions. The Communist Party is placed beyond good and evil, in fact it becomes that by which good and evil are to be judged.[9] We have also noted that some sectarians did fall into the same error as did the Communists. They claimed to have achieved the Kingdom upon earth. It would seem that so long as a group believes that the kingdom of God, or the perfect society, is to be built upon earth, the group is in continual danger of falling into tyrannical pretensions.

There is a dilemma here. If we abandon the idea of a perfect society upon earth, it is easy to sink into a complacent acceptance of what we have. The drive goes out of any hope for progress. The status quo is not called the kingdom of God, but since the Kingdom is unattainable, it is very easy to accept the present order as the best of all possible societies. The sectarians expressed a valid criticism of the churches that refused to work for a more Christian society. The churches expressed a valid criticism of the sects that believed the Kingdom was to come upon earth. Is there any way that we can express the validity of each without the weaknesses? It is imperative to find an answer to this question, for the whole

[9] See, for example, Friedrich Engels, Anti-Dühring, p. 104.

meaning of the Christian hope is involved. Let us, therefore, attempt a solution.

To be true to the Bible, the Christian view should realize that there is a sense in which the Kingdom is here now. This is the contribution which the Augustinian view makes to our solution. Modern scholarship has made it clear that Schweitzer's interpretation of the Kingdom as purely future, in Jesus' teachings, is a one-sided interpretation of only a part of the facts.[10] In a very real sense Jesus taught that the Kingdom had come with him and was present in his teachings and works. The purpose of life, therefore, is not simply in the future; it is here and now, and every individual can participate in this purpose. The Kingdom is the rule of God, which is eternal, but the earth remains a rebellious province of the Kingdom, so that the fulfillment of God's rule is still to be made manifest.[11] Since the coming of Jesus we live under the urgency of the Kingdom and participate in its meaning even as we work for its culmination.

In other words, there is a real sense in which the Kingdom is "beyond history." This phrase, "beyond history," made famous or infamous, depending upon your viewpoint, by the movement of neo-orthodoxy, may be an ambiguous phrase signifying nothing. It may be a new way of expressing the old Greek concept of escape from history. I believe, however, that it can be given a meaning that retains the validity of the sectarian view without its dangers.

[10] See F. C. Grant, *An Introduction to New Testament Thought* (New York and Nashville: Abingdon Press, 1950), pp. 154-57; A. N. Wilder, *Eschatology and Ethics in the Teaching of Jesus* (New York: Harper & Bros., 1950), chap. II; C. H. Dodd, *The Parables of the Kingdom* (London: Nisbet and Co., 1935), pp. 35-80.

[11] F. C. Grant, *The Gospel of the Kingdom* (New York: The Macmillan Co., 1940), p. xii.

"Beyond history" is a concept that should be closely connected with the doctrine of the resurrection of the body. These
two concepts mean that this life is not all that God has in
which to work his purpose with man. The biblical doctrine
of the resurrection of the body has been misunderstood by
most Christians and has been abandoned by many of them.
This is due primarily to the literal interpretation of it. Paul,
however, makes it clear that it is not to be taken literally. In
First Corinthians 15:35-50 he argues that the body is sown
material and is raised spiritual. The doctrine is best understood when it is set over against the idea that man has one
part of him, his soul, which is immortal and which shall slip
out of the body, at death, and be saved. If the soul is pure
and the body evil, then the soul cannot be helped toward
its salvation by what happens to the body. Against this the
Bible emphasizes the unity of man, body and soul. It is the
whole man who will live in the resurrection. Whatever happens to his bodily or historical existence is important and may
help or hinder his salvation. The resurrection of the body,
whatever else it may mean, implies that the resurrection is not
an escape from historical existence but a fulfillment of it. This
means that any moral victory won in this life has eternal
significance.

In the New Testament the concept of the coming Kingdom is used to express the faith that there is a dimension
of spiritual meaning in every event. The faith that one is in
relationship with that which is beyond space and time is
central to all religion. It escapes exact expression, however.
To say that the Other World is "close" implies spatial terms,
but we do not mean it spatially. The early Christians used the
concept of time rather than space, so that they said the
Kingdom was to come soon. What they were trying to say is

that the kingdom of God impinges upon life; it holds the meaning and goal of life. History is to find its meaning not in itself, but in the Kingdom. This truth can express itself in the hope of an apocalypse, but it can also express itself in the idea of a life after death. It is interesting to note that in the New Testament we can trace the shift from the one to the other. The kingdom of God of the Synoptics is being replaced by the "eternal life" of the Johannine literature. The shift is a legitimate one and in no way affects the essence of Christianity, since it is a purely symbolic change. But there is a danger in the change, particularly in the Greek world. When the symbol for the truth of the presence of God ceases to be apocalyptic and becomes life after death, you have the danger that the social nature of the Kingdom will be lost; you forget that history has a meaning and that history itself is to be used in the final consummation.

The change of symbol from apocalypse to eternal life opened the way to a dangerous perversion, which resulted in an otherworldly religion that sought to escape history. It was against such a religion that the sects rebelled. Yet the sects often made the mistake of transferring the symbol from that of life eternal to apocalypse in such a way that utopianism resulted.

There is a tension here in the Christian faith, as there is a tension in all profound insights into life. Because there is a tension, it runs the risk of becoming either a utopian hope for future history or an escape from history into otherworldliness. True Christianity is, I believe, neither. The kingdom of God which exists now impinges upon our whole life, filling it with meaning and pointing to a fulfillment of life and history. Because we are creatures of space and time, we have to put our ideas of that fulfillment in terms that imply the future. To God, who is beyond space and time, historical fulfillment is eternally present in every moment of time. God has a purpose for history, revealed in Christ, but the year 2154 will be no closer and no further from that purpose than the year 1954. If man does destroy himself in atomic warfare, this destruction will be opposed to the will of God, but it will not mean that God's purpose has been defeated; for that purpose has been at work fulfilling every moment of history.

This view seems to me to imply that death does not immediately send the "good" to heaven and the "evil" to hell. Such a view is essentially otherworldly and supposes that the historical existence, with its imperfections, is completely sloughed off. The resurrection of the body, as we have seen, seems to mean that man in his totality as a historical person will be raised. This means that his failings, the scars of history, will be upon him. He will be no more ready for immediate entry into the perfect Kingdom two seconds on the other side of death than he is two seconds on this side. Even those Christians who believe that perfection can be attained in this life admit that not many Christians do attain it. The battle of good and evil must continue until evil is put down and the forces of sin, which have made one unfit for life in the Kingdom, are purged away.

This is not a new or novel idea. It is at least as old as Origen and probably as old as the New Testament.[12] Protestantism, however, has always been very dubious of any such explanation, because it sounds like the purgatory of the Catholics,

---

[12] See I Cor. 15:22-29 and I Pet. 3:19, 4:6. The meaning of these passages is, of course, very obscure. However, my interpretation is in keeping with that of many scholars and seems somewhat more reasonable than any other alternative.

which Protestantism quite rightly repudiated. The doctrine of purgatory had given rise to a spiritual racket of buying souls. But in repudiating the abuses, Protestantism made a mistake in supposing that men were immediately divided into the good and the evil after death, although orthodox Protestantism, with its doctrine that the redeemed man is a redeemed sinner, has condemned the idea of trying to make such a division in this life.

A further Protestant objection is often the belief that such a view would tend to break down the conception of salvation by grace alone. But here too no contradiction is necessary. This is not to say that we must earn the Kingdom—it is still a gift of God—but it is to say that we must be made worthy to enter. This remains the work of God's grace. The kingdom of God is not a reward; it is the fellowship of the saints, and one must be made a saint or he cannot even appreciate being in it. There is something very profound in Bernard Shaw's discussion of heaven and hell in his *Man and Superman*. In one place Ana asks the Devil if she or anybody can go to heaven if they wish, and the Devil replies contemptuously that she can, if her tastes lie in that direction.[13] This implies what I am trying to say here, that to enter the Kingdom one must be schooled in the ways of the Kingdom, or he would not choose to be there.

This interpretation of the fulfillment of history beyond history implies that history is of supreme value. In history the lives are being formed which are to be "resurrected." The historical situation, being a fallen and sinful condition, is not a good school for the Kingdom. Anything which creates barriers that divide man from man is creating barriers that will

[13] Act III.

outlast life. In Jesus' parable, the gulf which was formed between Dives and Lazarus during their lives continued to separate them in the afterlife. So it is with the gulfs between men which are dug by nationalism, racial prejudices, individual pride, unequal power—they have eternal significance. All of these must be overcome before the Kingdom is perfected and history fulfilled. Hence as we fight the social evils which dig these gulfs, we are preparing men for the Kingdom; we are fighting the battle of Armageddon. These historical tasks are not to be shunned or ignored; they have eternal significance.

But the Christian knows that no achievement in this life can equal the kingdom of God. This life must continue to have imperfections of sin within it. Thus no claims to a false righteousness may be made in the name of any historical achievements as they are made in the name of the Communist achievements in Russia. Christians too are guilty of self-righteousness, but at least when they are, they know that they are in opposition to the faith which tells them that all things must be kept under the judgment of God. History does not achieve perfection, but history must strive toward perfection. This is why the Christian can work to save history even when he sees no evidence of salvation within history. He knows that his work, however small, if it is for the Kingdom, will have its final culmination and significance when God's kingdom is completed.

Precisely because he does not demand an earthly or historical fulfillment of his work, the Christian is likely to accomplish more historical good than those who hope only for historical fulfillment and thus run the dangers of fanatic self-righteousness or disillusioned despair. The greatest contributions to world peace may well be made not by those who believe that if man destroys himself in atomic war, there will be nothing left, but by the Christian who does not need history to fulfill the meaning of his life. He may make the greatest contribution precisely because he can afford to be realistic about the possibilities and will not be led away by fanaticism into blind alleys.

Here, I submit, is a Christian alternative to the utopianism that is implicit in the sectarians and explicit in the Communists. This utopianism leads the one to an ineffectual attack upon society and the other to demonic pretension of having achieved the Kingdom in a very relative world situation. This Christian answer has resources which enable it to escape such errors. It takes history seriously but does not see it as an ultimate.

LOSS OF VALUE OF THE INDIVIDUAL IN COMMUNISM

One of the concepts of Christianity which is glossed over in Marx and repudiated by Communist societies is the value of the individual. Actually the belief in the value of each individual originated in the biblical revelation and cannot have any secure basis outside that tradition. It is based upon the belief that man is valuable because there is a God who loves him and to whom he is valuable. If you take away the God who gives man his value, you have no objectivity for the value. It is impossible to show that men are, in any measurable way, equal. Science can only show the inequality of man. Some philosophers have suggested the "greatest good of the greatest number" as an adequate substitute. This is a perverse mistake. The "greatest good of the greatest number" is, by itself, neither Christian nor democratic; it is essentially totalitarian. Every totalitarian atrocity of this century has been committed in the name of this principle. It sacrifices the individual to the mob.

The Christian doctrine is that each individual has basic rights, and it is not a mathematical question at all. Just because you can add up numbers against an individual, you do not thereby make him any less important, nor do you take from him his rights.

If nature is ultimate, it is perfectly logical for a naturalistic ethic to begin with the ruthlessness of nature. Nature is prodigal with individual lives, but the species is cherished. When this principle of nature is made the principle of history, there can be no hesitancy in making the individual into a means for an end, provided the end is the welfare of the group as a whole. This is just what Communism does with its "scientific ethic."

Communism lacks any basis for giving a value to man as an individual. It looks upon man as a creature of space and time, wholly confined therein. Man's problems are to be solved in a purely natural and material way by a change in the social structure, not by a change in the individual. Death is not taken with sufficient seriousness, for the death of the individual is ignored as a problem. As a result, there is no ultimate value to the life of the individual.

For Marx the class was always more real than the individual. He saw not Tom Smith or Henry Jones, but a proletarian or a capitalist. The meaning of history was tied up solely with classes. The important thing to Marx was never what happened to the individual but what happened to the class. The important thing was for the proletariat to rise and the capitalists to fall, regardless of what it might cost individuals in the process.

This emphasis upon the class rather than upon the individual means that freedom is thought of in terms of class freedom rather than individual freedom. The individual must fit himself as best he can into the collective whole, which is, supposedly, free. Whereas Christianity demands the right of each individual to be free because of his individual relationship to God, Communism thinks only of the class's being free in relation to the abolition of other classes.

The consequence of these views of man and of the views of history discussed in the previous section, is that the individual becomes a means to an end. All moral considerations in Communism are resolved down to a question of whether or not a certain action will help or hinder the achievement of the Marxian goal. Thus the proletarian welfare may demand that any number of former Party faithful be "physically liquidated," that peasants be starved, that Koreans be thrown into war. All things become moral when the essential sacredness of the individual is lost, and nothing is left as a principle but the hope of a class victory.

Yet the paradox of Communism is that it needs just such a doctrine of the value of the individual. The whole condemnation of capitalism is built around the way in which it dehumanizes the individual. As Dean Inge has pointed out:

"From each according to his ability, to each according to his needs." This is the fundamental principle of Communism. The claim of the worker is not based on the value of his work, but simply on the ground that he exists. The appeal is not economic, but sentimental or humanitarian.[14]

If the individual is not of ultimate importance, why

[14] H. W. Harris, ed., *Christianity and Communism* (Oxford: Basil Blackwell, 1937), p. 12.

should he receive according to his needs? But if he is of ultimate importance, why should he be treated as a pawn in the class struggle? This remains a basic contradiction at the heart of Communism.

FAILURE TO UNDERSTAND SIN AND FORGIVENESS

At first sight it may seem to be a contradiction to make the charge that Communism fails to understand sin, since it has already been praised, in the last chapter, for understanding the sinful nature of human institutions. It is true that, compared with a sentimental liberalism, Communism understands very well that all human actions and ideals are colored by self-interest, or as Marx would say, class interest. Similarly, Communism believes that injustice necessarily follows in the wake of undue privilege or economic power. With all of this the Christian doctrine of sin would agree. Nevertheless, Communism makes the disastrous mistake of believing that sin is the result of social organization.

Communism sees man as essentially good, but perverted by the social system. Men are divided into classes, with which their interests are involved and which they defend at all cost of truth or justice. The solution, for Communism, is to change the economic system so that the classes are abolished. This is brought out in Marx's dream of a future anarchistic Utopia when the state shall wither away because it has nothing to do. The predatory aspects of man will no longer be expressed. Sin, being the result of the social system, will disappear when the perfect social system is built.

History and any profound study of man reveal, I believe, the essential truth of the Christian view of sin and the sentimentality of Communism at this point. By sin we mean the tendency of man to seek and preserve his own interests at the expense of his fellow men. We mean the fact that man is self-centered and tends to see the world from the limited perspective of his own group. This means that his claims to righteousness are always, in part, pretensions. It means that he refuses to place himself under God's judgment but places instead some creation of his own in the position of the absolute so that by its judgments he may appear as righteous. Call these tendencies what you will, they are what the Christian faith has meant by sin. They are a continual and perennial danger to human society, and they appear in all men. These sinful tendencies are not to be left behind with an old society when a new one is entered.

The one point that the Communists have never been able to explain is that, if man is essentially good and society creates evil, how does it happen that society fell from its original righteousness? The Communist parrots that a change in the means of production occurred which made some men owners and some men slaves. But a change in production could not do this unless there was already within man a desire to be a master.

Herbert Butterfield, a historian, throws considerable light on the problem of the origin of social sin when he points out that if social forces of repression are abandoned, normally respectable men become predatory aggressors, having no fear to restrain them. He concludes:

It is not social institutions that make men worse than they might have been. . . . Social institutions, however bad, are better than nothing and have the effect of making men appear a little more virtuous than they really are. . . .

We may begin by saying that only some men—only a few

very bad people—are egotistical. . . . We may begin by arguing
that it was the selfishness of the capitalists which was to blame. . . .
Then we note how the friends of the workers become alive to the
fact that the capitalists were taking advantage of the competitive
spirit, the rival cupidities amongst the wage-earners themselves.[15]

This would indicate that sin is something which social change
alone cannot overcome.

Communism is left with a basic contradiction. Unless there
are in man tendencies to sin, then man would not have made
use of changes in production to exploit his fellow men. But
if there are such tendencies in man, what is to prevent man in
the Communist society from using opportunities in the new
order to oppress his fellows? For example, what will prevent
the dictatorship of the proletariat from being used by a few
to exalt themselves at the expense of society? Marx never
faced this question, but that it is a question is proved by
developments in Russia, where the dictatorship of the proletariat has become the dictatorship of the party and hence the
dictatorship of a bureaucracy.

Marx's great mistake lies in thinking that the actions of
man are based upon economic needs alone. Because man
lacks economic security, he tries to secure himself at the expense of his fellow men. Marx thought man could be cured
of this tendency when the Communist system had removed
the insecurities from the economic sphere. Man would then
have no further reason to exalt himself. Marx was quite right
in seeing that so long as men are starving, economic needs
are their first concern. He failed, however, to see that the
needs of men are not just physical and economic but are also
spiritual. Thus what man desires always outreaches his grasp.

[15] *Christianity and History* (New York: Charles Scribner's Sons, 1950),
pp. 34-36. Used by permission of the publishers.

When he gains economic security, he finds that he "needs" power and prestige. Much of the money-making in our society has long since ceased to be economic at all; it is simply a means of gaining power and position. In any society conflicts will arise. A group dedicated to noneconomic ends, such as art clubs, social clubs, churches, can have as many conflicts over prestige and position as there are economic conflicts in society at large. Marx saw the conflict of past history but made the mistake of thinking that it could not occur in a communistic society. Nonetheless, it has happened in Russia. Classes have appeared in a new form and have used any means at their disposal to exalt themselves. No state has been used more exclusively in the interests of a class than the Russian state has been used in the interests of the bureaucracy.

Several consequences follow from this failure of judgment. First of these is the tendency of the Communists to fear economic power but to fail to see the dangers of political power. Yet the one is as dangerous as the other, since any form of power is a means whereby man can express his desire to subjugate others. Political power is just as dangerous as economic. Marx saw that too much economic power means that the holders of that power will exploit others. He nonetheless blithely believed that political power could be given to the proletariat or Communist Party and that this power would wither away. Marx knew that you could not appeal to the conscience of the capitalists and have them give up their power, yet he thought that the Communist bureaucrats would do just that. But Russia has proved that there is no solution for the problems of man by taking the power from the capitalists and giving it to the commissars. To quote Trotsky again:

However you may interpret the nature of the present Soviet State, one thing is indubitable; at the end of its second decade of existence, it has not only not died away, but not begun to die away. Worse than that, it has grown into a hitherto unheard apparatus of compulsion.[16]

Yet Trotsky does not see that there is anything wrong with Marx's analysis. He blames the perverseness of the rulers of Russia but not the ideas upon which he, as they, had built.

Mankind remains in a continual dilemma. Economic justice cannot be obtained without political power. But political power is as dangerous as the economic. The Christian understanding of man is thus suspicious of both capitalism and communism. It knows the possibilities of perversion in both. Christianity is essentially democratic; for it knows that only when power is distributed as widely as possible among all the people, can we escape in some measure the exploitation of man by man. Reinhold Niebuhr has performed a great service in pointing out that the Christian believes in democracy not because all men are naturally good enough to govern, but because no man is good enough to have in his hands unchecked power.[17]

A second consequence of the Communist error about human nature is self-righteousness. Communists have a doctrine which sees clearly the sin in others but never the sin in themselves. Any criticism of their activities, therefore, is obviously a clear example of fascism, reaction, Trotskyism, or some other perverse attitude. This has made for great practical difficulties in the Communist Party. Their refusal to look critically at themselves has often cost them support that they

[16] Op. cit., p. 51. Used by permission of Pioneer Publishers.
[17] See particularly his Children of Light and the Children of Darkness (New York: Charles Scribner's Sons, 1944).

might otherwise have gained. Of course, there is a spirit of self-criticism in the Party which at first sight seems to contradict this statement, but the criticism moves in narrow circles. It cannot criticize the "Party line" itself; it can only ask to what degree the Party line is being followed or missed.

Similarly, the achievements of the Communists, in particular the achievements of the Soviet state in Russia, are forever and always above judgment. Again, criticism is allowed, but it remains in the narrow realm of petty questions. As André Gide sums it up: "What really interests them [Russian people] is to know whether we admire them enough. What they are afraid of is that we should be ill informed as to their merits. What they want from us is not information but praise." [18]

The point is, of course, that when you get a communist society, sin must be gone. This is what Marxism teaches. Anyone who would suggest that a communist society could sin is obviously unmarxian.

Such a spirit of complacency can never lead to a vital or progressive society. Strangely enough, the radical and revolutionary Communist becomes a conservative of the conservatives after the revolution, because he refuses to admit that there might be any necessity for further reform or revolution. Perfection has been found. This is not to suggest that Communists have any monopoly on self-righteousness. All groups and individuals are cursed with it in some degree. The Communists, however, have a theory which justifies their self-righteousness and makes it inevitable.

A consequence of this self-righteous attitude is that the Communists have no mercy or understanding for their op-

[18] Return from the U.S.S.R., tr. Dorothy Bussey (New York: Alfred A. Knopf, 1937), p. 31.

ponents. Because they do not see themselves stained with the same sin as their enemies, the Communists have no love for them. Marx could declare that the capitalist was determined by his economic position to be what he was. And still Marx could heap upon the same capitalist all of his venom and hate. It was the typical blindness of the self-righteous. Marx's followers have ruthlessly exterminated all opposition and wiped out heretical elements within the Party with no sign of sympathy for their victims. There is no room for such sympathy in the Communist system, for it is a system of black and white.

Throughout all Christian views of man and history there runs the theme of forgiveness. Because of the Christian understanding of sin, the Christian knows that he needs to be forgiven by God. Before he can stand in the presence of the Almighty, the Christian must confess, "I am sinful and unclean, I have fallen short of thy glory." When a man has undergone the humiliating sense of being forgiven, he should have his heart softened toward the sin of others. Having tackled the plank in his own eye, he is more gentle with the splinter in the eye of his neighbor. It is probably not an overstatement to claim that no man will be completely forgiving of the sins of others until he has recognized his own sin and sought forgiveness for it. Self-complacency and self-righteousness are incompatible with a forgiving heart.

The humility that is necessary for the Christian experience of forgiveness is scorned by our secular world. The secularist finds nothing before which he may legitimately bow himself in humble penitence. But the Christian believes in a God whose righteousness and holiness are such that he is deserving of man's repentance. At this point we find one of the features that divide the sects from the Communists and put the former clearly into the camp of the Christians.

Most sectarians had the Christian understanding of their own need of repentance and forgiveness. They were not led to any idea that some form of social organization was going to free man from his sin. The sects may have had their self-righteous moments (and we shall see later that herein lies a fault of theirs), but they did, at their best, always know that it was not they who judged themselves, but God who judged them. While they did heap vindictiveness upon the heads of their enemies, even as the Communists do, they were not without consciousness of the Christian command to forgive their enemies. There runs through the sectarian literature a sense of concern for the souls of the very men who were persecuting them. George Fox the Younger is typical of sectarian Christianity as he pours out his heart in the plea, "Oh! that the rulers that now are would be persuaded (whilst they have their day) by the Lord . . . to receive the Lord Jesus Christ to be their king and teacher. . . . But alas how few there are that will hear." [19] Such a plea is strange to Marx. Marx might hope that some of the bourgeoisie would join the proletariat, but he was thinking of the value they would be to the proletariat, not the value it would be to the bourgeois.

Many sectarians, however, did make the mistake of thinking that sin and the need for continual forgiveness could be overcome in this life, by the sects themselves. The sects were quite rightly concerned over the complacency which the orthodox church revealed in the presence of its sins. They saw the doctrine of original sin being used to justify un-

[19] *Op. cit.*, p. 210.

christian living. The sects went wrong, however, when they assumed too easily that man could attain perfection. George Fox can barely contain his anger as he condemns the idea that perfection is not a possibility for the Christian. He says, "Hath not all you [the priests and ministers] crying up sin, while men are upon the earth, [meant that] they must never be free from sin; and is not this come from the whore's cup?" [20] This belief can lead to a new self-righteousness, and Fox himself came close to it when he said, "I knew nothing but pureness and innocency and righteousness, being renewed in the image of Christ Jesus so that I say I was come up to the state of Adam, which he was in before he fell." [21]

In the sects this trend toward self-righteousness is modified by a sense of having God in judgment over one's life, and while it often led to pharisaical pride, it did not exist without sharp checks upon it. But when we find the same note in the secularized "sect" of Communism, it has become absolute. The righteous are the workers of the world. They can do no wrong so long as they follow their Communist leaders. The basis has been laid for the most extreme claims of self-righteousness and pretension. The Communists always miss the paradox of the ethical life. The "good" lose their goodness by making claims to a greater righteousness than is theirs. The biblical Pharisees did have a moral standard and attainment higher than that of their time, and yet they lost that relative righteousness by claiming a complete righteousness, which blinded them to their shortcomings. This happens wherever men divide the world into the good and evil with a simple but sharp line of demarcation. This results in the

[20] Collected Works, IV, 188.
[21] Quoted by Reinhold Niebuhr, Nature and Destiny of Man (New York: Charles Scribner's Sons, 1945), II, 170.

"good" losing the goodness that they did have to begin with.

I pointed out before that the poor, the oppressed, do have a real righteousness in their claims against society. In fighting for their own good, they are fighting for a greater justice. But the fatal trap is that such groups will come to see themselves as more righteous than they really are, will fail to see themselves stained with the same sin that stains their enemies. When they come to power, therefore, they claim to have wiped out all the evils which they attacked in the old society. Actually they often repeat in a new form the sins of the age which they have overcome.

This is illustrated in those followers of Cromwell who, dividing the world into good and bad, destroyed the "bad." Then they set up the new parliament in the image of the old king and the presbytery in the image of the old bishop. There was some gain in justice, but by no means the absolute gain for which they had fought and which they claimed to have achieved. Similarly in Russia, the revolution by the "righteous" proletariat resulted in setting up Stalin and the bureaucracy in place of the tsar, the Communist Party in the place of the old nobility, and yet the proletariat was able to believe that it had achieved the perfection of history.

The biblical point of view recognizes that all men have sinned and come short of God's glory, that the redeemed man is a forgiven sinner who will need to be forgiven again and again. This means that the evil which we fight in others is to be found in ourselves also. It enables us to see that, no group being free of sin, there is no social advance which is not in danger. Freedom once gained can be lost. There can be no continual and steady progress, but only an eternal battle against the forces of evil which would corrupt every society, including the Church, and every historical attainment. It means that the Christian does not spend his time looking at enemies outside his country, his church, his political party, or himself. He knows too well that the same evils arise from within each of these. The paradoxical but true insight of Pascal is that there are only two kinds of people, the sinners who believe that they are righteous and the righteous who know that they are sinners. True righteousness, the kind that can keep free of pretension, is precisely that which knows its own sinfulness. Yet because sinfulness is partly self-deception, no one ever attains complete righteousness.

The Christian must humbly remember that he is falling short of God's will, that the moment he claims perfection he has become a pharisee. But at the same time he must remember Jesus' demand that his righteousness is to exceed that of the Pharisees. We do not overcome pharisaism by ceasing to aim for perfection. This tension can only be overcome by the deeply Christian experience of salvation by grace. We have no right to boast of our achievements or to feel superior, for the grace of God alone has made us what we are. The Christian has achieved his position before God not because he was good enough to earn it, but because he was freely forgiven by God's love. Salvation by grace includes the experience of forgiveness, and from this comes the strength, not our own, whereby those things that are impossible with man are made possible by God (Matt. 19:26).

In conclusion, I hope that this section has brought out an important point. We had seen that one cause of Marxian tyranny is its lack of a suprahistorical basis of judgment or a suprahistorical goal in life. In view of the tendency of some of the sects to fall into self-righteousness, however, we can also see that belief in God is not enough, in itself, to save a group from tyrannical pretensions. It may even increase such pretensions when, as at Munster, the sect is identified with the will of God. Belief in God must be united with the Christian doctrine of sin and forgiveness, sometimes obscured by the sects, if it is to escape tyrannical implications. These doctrines understand that the "righteous" or "Christian" man is not freed completely from self-interest and pretension. This means that he may not be trusted to make righteous use of unlimited powers, nor may he identify his acts with the will of God.

The Christian doctrine of sin must always be balanced by the Christian doctrines of forgiveness and the new life. To take the doctrine of sin alone leads to despair. Overwhelmed with the thought that one cannot escape sin, a man may cease striving to come closer to perfection. That is, he forgets that the forgiving grace of God offers a new life "in Christ" to him. On the other hand, the doctrine of the new life through forgiving grace, by itself, may cause a man to forget that he is still a sinner. The two doctrines, held together, are able to preserve a man from both pitfalls.

The Augustinian theology has, at its best, preserved both facets of Christian faith. But when it errs, it is likely to err in the direction of overemphasizing the doctrine of sin and forgetting the new power that comes from the experience of forgiveness. "Barthian" theology at times seems to do this, as its emphasis upon sin tends to obscure the gospel promise that sin, under the grace of God, may be overcome. The sectarian view, at its best, preserved both facets. But when it erred, it was likely to overemphasize the power of forgiveness and the new life so that it forgot the continuing nature of sin. We saw this illustrated in George Fox's claim to have attained the perfection from which Adam fell. The two Christian traditions, therefore, act as a balance to each other.

In the light of their combined testimony we can see clearly
the flaws that led Communism to totalitarian pretensions.

CONCLUSION

Despite the fact that Communism has certain truths with
which Christianity agrees, we find that Christianity in both
the church and sect types of its thought is basically opposed
to Communism. Even when, in its sectarian form, Christianity had close parallels with Communism, the differences were
more fundamental. This chapter has, I hope, made this fact
clear. Christians maintain that man is built upon dimensions
that history cannot exhaust. Consequently, Christians do not
think that time can save man. They believe that only God,
who is beyond time, can do this. Furthermore, they know
that historical forces cannot save man, for the historical
forces themselves stand in need of salvation.

In this Christian faith, the individual stands out as the
son of God with rights and privileges. Yet, even as sons of
God, men fall into sin which is not to be overcome lightly or
easily. Each man has to face up to and overcome his own problems, and a change in society, by itself, will not save him. The
sectarian revolt against the church was, in large part, the
revolt against the idea that a man could be made good by
being born into a good society, and this revolt is a vital part
of the Christian faith.

It would seem that it was the Christian element of the
sects which enabled them, in co-operation with Christians of
the church type, to contribute so much to the founding of
modern democracy. It was the theology common to all Christians but scorned by the Communists, who otherwise praise
the sects, that enabled the sects to speak a word for freedom
and democracy which Communists have not yet been able

to speak. This theology aided them in understanding the value and nature of man as well as the central problems of history. It saved most of them from idolatrous loyalty to a particular regime, which always leads to tyranny.

Of course, as we have pointed out, some of the sects were led to a new philosophy of tyranny by their belief that they were the chosen agents of God to set up and rule the Kingdom. Likewise, church types, overlooking injustice, often have absolutized the *status quo* of a given point in history. But where this has occurred, new voices have arisen to remind Christians again that all men are under the judgment of God and that all historical situations fall short of the Kingdom for which they pray. And ever behind the judgment of God there lies a word of hope. The Christian knows that he is not alone in the struggle to rid the world of the evils that are out of harmony with the spirit of the Kingdom. No deed performed in the service of Christ, however small or seemingly futile, will be without its significance in God's final victory. No life lived in the service of Christ will have been lived in vain.

WHEN CHRISTIANITY AND COMMUNISM MEET

OUR study of Communism leads us to quote with approval John Bennett's statement that "Communism as a faith and as a system of thought is a compound of half-truth and positive error." [1] This statement does not say that Communism is a dubious thing, fairly good; it says that Communism is essentially evil. But it also recognizes that it is dangerously powerful because that positive error can make use of the half-truth to win followers and to influence world affairs. There are many who would like to hide their eyes from the half-truth and concentrate upon the positive error. They insist that any admission of the half-truth would be to give comfort to the enemy. But to me it seems that to deny the half-truth gives an even greater power to the movement and enables it to win more followers. Not to agree with Communism when it is right is to alienate completely those people who know that it does have a half-truth.

What I have tried to show is that Christianity has also this truth which Communism has. The sectarians help to prove this. But I have tried also to show that in Christianity this half-truth does not need to be mixed with the same positive error.

When we use the word "communism" in today's world, we need to recognize that it includes two elements which must be separated. First, there is the historic meaning of

[1] Christianity and Communism (New York: Association Press, 1948), p. 9.

the word, wherein is pictured the ideal society, in which all injustices would be overcome, a society in which "mine" and "thine" would be replaced by "ours." It would be a society in which men would be finally and truly brothers. This ideal has haunted the greatest minds of men, from Plato to the present. It was practiced by the early Christians and preached by the sects. It is, in reality, the vision of the kingdom of God upon earth, which is a vital part of the Christian message. This ideal society has never dawned and will never dawn upon earth during the history of man. Yet it remains eternally valid as the ideal goal, the star to which society can hitch its wagon. No society ever dares to remove itself from the judgment of this ideal; no society can hold to it without being uplifted and improved. For this reason the Church must continue to pray, "Thy Kingdom come," and to preach the implications of these radical words.

The second meaning of "communism" refers to that modern movement begun by Marx and Engels and developed by Lenin and Stalin. This is a revolutionary movement, with totalitarian undertones, that has become the right arm of Russian imperialism. As such the Communist movement is a threat to the freedom and spiritual values of man. Its militant atheism, which hides a naïve idolatry, its materialistic values, its class hatred, and its resort to violent revolution put it in opposition to Christianity. Nevertheless, it lays claim to being the true inheritor of the traditional communistic idealism outlined above.

Not only does the modern Russian Communist movement pay lip service to these traditional ideals, but it also, when in power, makes certain overtures toward putting some of them into practice. If challenged that it ought to put more of them into practice, it has the convenient excuse that this is still the period of the dictatorship of the proletariat and that the real communism is to come.

When we understand these two meanings of communism, we can understand a great many other things. For example, we can understand the many sincere and idealistic persons who have fallen prey to the "Party line." They really believed in the idealistic communism and have been misled to think that Marxian Communism was putting these ideals into practice. The great disillusionment of these people comes when they realize that Marxian Communism, organized under Russia, is really the greatest threat to the idealistic society of which they dream.

This also helps us to understand certain elements of fanatical opposition to Communism. Many people who are opposed to Communism are not really shocked at its totalitarianism nor at its denials of freedom. They are shocked rather at its claim to be putting into practice the ideals of brotherhood and equality. This is proved by the fact that they are not unduly anxious to wipe out the evils of fascism. These people often reveal themselves in their true light by supporting the Ku Klux Klan or semifascist movements. They may, however, hide this feeling under the pious expression of democratic, and even Christian, ideals. Christians, in their opposition to Communism, must beware of becoming allied with such groups.

This also aids us in understanding the great appeal which Communism makes to certain areas of the world today. Wherever there is injustice, hunger, imperialism, racial discrimination, or any other glaring inequality, there the Communists' claim that they represent equality and justice will be heard gladly. People in despair are not likely to examine closely any movement which promises to right all their wrongs and remove their troubles. But wherever such situations exist, there Christianity has failed to be Christian. Every time Communism takes over a new territory, it is a judgment upon all who claim to follow Christ; we have failed to banish the evils which Communism uses as steppingstones to power. We must fight Communism by making Christianity work.

Marxian Communism is usually called a movement of radicalism or of the "Left," and it would like to pass under this guise. Such a movement is what many people are looking for in those areas where the status quo is intolerable. Communism lays its claim to being radical upon its lip service to the ideals of historic communism. In actual practice, it is reactionary. Its way is not a step forward from democratic society as we know it, but a long step backward. True progressive radicalism today is nowhere better expressed than in the pronouncements of Christianity, particularly as they appear in the great ecumenical documents of the World Council of Churches.

These Christian principles include a refusal to give absolute blessing to any particular form of social or economic structure and an insistence upon justice, security, and equality in combination with freedom. They are truly radical because they recognize and seek to overcome concentrated power, whether it be political power (Communism), economic power (monopoly capitalism), or ecclesiastical power. Insofar as these Christian principles prevail, Marxian Communism will be impotent to ensnare the minds and hearts of men.

In this study I have tried to demonstrate that there is much substance to the oft-repeated statement that Communism is a religion. In showing its parallels to the sects, I hope that I have added illustrative material to this statement. Of course, the statement could be denied by defining religion in some way so that Communism was ruled out. Even then we would say that Communism means to Communists what "religion" means to the "religious." It gives them a purpose in life, claims their ultimate allegiance, and gives them hope of powers greater than themselves which are carrying them to their chosen goals. That is, if we do not call Communism a religion, we must call it a substitute for religion.

If Communism is a religion, or a substitute for religion, it means that only by a religious attack can it be overcome. Paganism was not overcome by the rationalism of the Greek philosophers, but by the religion of Christianity. The same story has been repeated continually throughout history. The religion of Communism is strong today precisely because so much of the world finds itself in a religious vacuum. The Communist religion sounds scientific, makes many of the promises made by orthodox religion, and hence partially fills the vacuum for many persons.

If Communism is a religion, we may well ask why a society dominated by Christianity turned to this new religious faith? I believe that we will find that this was partly because of the failures of Christianity in the areas of the half-truth of Communism. Because Christianity has sat unheeding in the midst of injustice and oppression, the Communists could make their half-truth seem like the whole truth. Because Christians have not made more of society Christian, because the Church has too often been allied with powerful and wealthy classes, the Communists have moved into the very working groups with which Christianity began. It is not enough to condemn the evils of Communism; Christianity must repent of its own failures and try to overcome them while yet there is time.

Among other things, our Christian culture must confess that its opposition to Communism has been much less effective than it might have been. This is because so much of our world has accepted the essence of the Communist philosophy. In fact, Communism seems, in many ways, to be nothing but one particularly unruly expression of the modern view of life. While condemning Communistic "materialism" in theory, the rest of the world has lived by materialistic motives. The Communists have been hated primarily because they have dragged the skeleton from the closet of Western culture. While the West has lived quite complacently upon the unspoken assumption that the greatest goal in life is to amass material wealth, the Communists, with their theory of economic determinism, have shouted this belief from the housetops.

Our Western world has been in the process of becoming more and more secular for centuries—in fact, if not in theory. Our idea of history has built largely upon the hope of a continual progress based upon science, education, and democracy. Progress has meant primarily a chicken in every pot and two cars in every garage. We have blithely assumed that with this increase in material wealth there will come peace, mental health, and brotherly fellowship among men. Like the Communists we have looked for the goal of history within history, and like the Communists we have tended to make the men of the present into means for the future. Like the Communists we have lived in the faith that life gains meaning from the fact that history will find its culmination before the earthly life of mankind is completed. It follows from this, for us as for the Communists, that any means are justified if they contribute to the end of the coming era of earthly bliss.

We have become very apologetic about anything that sounds "otherworldly." It is played down even in our churches. We shrink from suggesting that man needs power from be-

yond himself to aid him in his struggles. We have believed
that all man needs to do is to roll up his sleeves and tackle
his problems. Any idea that this life points beyond itself to
another and fuller life has been played down. It is mentioned
only at funeral services, where it might give some temporary
comfort to the bereaved until they can overcome their grief
by losing themselves in the getting and spending of life. We
have been frightened by the Communist jibe that we are
offering "pie in the sky" to dull the demand for social justice.

The time has come to challenge this prevailing view of the
West. The Communists do not offer pie in the sky, but they
do offer pie the day after tomorrow, when the heavenly Utopia
of Communism will be born. Heaven has never been used
more exclusively to persuade people to accept meekly the
present injustices than the Communists have used their dream
of a future earthly bliss. In an age like ours, the Communist
form of opiate sounds more attractive and hence is more effective than the promise of an afterlife.

In the light of this situation, it comes as a shock to read
that, if present rates of growth continue during the next ten
years, the Soviet Union may be able to supply a higher standard of living to its citizens than western Europe. Furthermore, even the United States may be overtaken in the not-too-
distant future.[2] Faced with this prospect, we suddenly realize
how much of our popular defense against Communism has
been built upon the argument that the Western world has a
higher standard of living than the Communists. Conservatives have argued against Communism by pointing to the fact
that while Russian workers, in theory, own the factories in
which they work, it is the American worker who, in fact,

drives his own automobile. Liberals have argued that the best way to defeat Communism abroad is to feed more people faster than the Communists can. Such arguments begin to look a little dubious in face of a rapidly expanding Russian economy.

I believe that I have said enough to demonstrate my belief that social justice is a necessary part of the Christian answer to Communism. Wherever hunger and injustice exist, the Christian cannot be unconcerned. But social justice is not the whole answer. Even if Communism should prove able to give a higher standard of living than the free world, there are basic reasons why the Christian must continue to set his face against the movement. Communism does not do justice to the integrity and value of the individual; its philosophy of history is too shallow.

Actually, I do not believe that the materialistic values of Communism are its most persuasive. It is our own implicit materialism which makes us fear them. There is no evidence that the world has been won to Americanism by the fact of America's high standard of living, and it would seem unlikely that Communism would have any more success through the means of offering a greater abundance of material things. It is quite probable that in recent years the Communist claims to stand for peace and racial equality have won more followers than Communist promises of greater material benefits. We are told that in Asiatic countries one of the greatest lures of Communism is its picture of a more brotherly society. This is particularly the case in India, where there is not as high an evaluation put upon material wealth as in America.

In short, it is as a religion, giving meaning and hope to life, that Communism is most dangerous. Communism calls fanatical followers to work for a better world. In this crusade

they find a meaning and destiny for themselves. They find
the promise that their work will be fulfilled in the coming
victory of Communism. At the same time Christianity stirs
millions of its followers to nothing more than a mild aesthetic
experience once a week. If we lose the struggle with Communism, it will not be because we have been outproduced;
it will be because we have been less dedicated and less inspired by our religious faith than the Communist world.

I am not, however, pessimistic. I believe that the Communist philosophy lacks profundity; it cannot reach the
heights or the depths of man's nature. Communism is a
half-truth, and eventually every half-truth destroys itself by
its own inherent contradiction. It cannot ultimately satisfy
the deepest needs of man's life. When man asks for bread,
Communism claims to be able to give him bread in abundance, and too often the Church has given but the stone of
indifference. But man does not live by bread alone, and
Communism will fail when men finally begin to hunger and
thirst after a higher righteousness. When man is driven again
to face the ultimate questions—"What must I do to inherit
eternal life?" "Where is Abundant Life?" "What is the meaning of life?"; Christianity will again prove to be the more sufficient answer.

Marx, seeing only man's economic drives, ignored his spiritual needs. Whole societies, not all of them Communist,
have been built upon this viewpoint. In fact, it has been
argued with some cogency that Marx's thinking at this point
was made plausible by the nature of the capitalistic society in
which he lived. It was a society which had become so pre-
occupied with the economic that it is not strange that a
system of thought should be built around it. And so, building
upon this theory, societies have appeared which gave man

his pie upon earth, but a woman leaps from a window to escape the Communist heaven and flees to the arms of a branch of the historical Church. Her act is symbolic of the fact that, although man cannot be satisfied with his "pie" in the sky, neither, it seems, can he be satisfied with "heaven" upon earth.

This study, if valid, means that, in the final analysis, the only manner in which Communism can be overcome is by a positive attack. Too much anti-Communism has been just that—anti-Communism. It has not had a positive alternative to offer. A purely negative approach is not enough against a dynamically positive religion like Communism. Christianity has, I believe, just the message the times call for. We need the positive, dynamic voice of Christianity with its radical note of judgment; but it must be judgment not only upon Communism, but also upon those failures of democracy and Christianity which have enabled the half-truth of Communism to capture so many hungry millions. We need the hope of Christianity to meet the hopes inspired by Communism, but it must be presented as hope for all men and not just for the favored few in the future, be that future here or hereafter. We need the message of Christ that forgiveness and a new life are a possibility both for individuals and society. We need the Christian conviction that every man is of infinite value because he is a son of God regardless of his class or race. In short, we need the full gospel of Christ to overcome the gospel of Marx.

During the Second World War a writer in a popular magazine commented upon the fact that while the Nazis believed all the wrong things with fanatical zeal, the Western world believed all the right things but without any great enthusiasm. It is this problem that haunts modern Christianity as it stands face to face with Communism. Can we, at this eleventh hour, find again the springs of motivation that have caused Christians time and time again to overturn the world? If we can, Communism will have met more than its match. The time has come for Christians to cease apologizing for their gospel and to start living it. Communist fanaticism must be met by Christian enthusiasm.

INDEX